Class, Gender, and the American Family Farm in the 20th Century

Integrating a focus on gender with Marx's surplus-based notion of class, this book offers a one-of-a-kind analysis of family farms in the United States. The analysis shows how gender and class struggles developed during important moments in the history of these family farms and how they shaped the trajectory of U.S. agricultural development. It also generates surprising insights about the family farm we thought we knew, as well as the food and agricultural system today.

Elizabeth A. Ramey theorizes the family farm as a complex hybrid of mostly feudal and ancient class structures. This class-based definition of the family farm yields unique insights into three broad aspects of U.S. agricultural history. First, the analysis highlights the crucial, yet under-recognized, role of farm women's and children's unpaid labor in subsidizing the family farm. Second, it allows for a new, class-based perspective on the roots of the twentieth century "miracle of productivity" in U.S. agriculture. Lastly, the book demonstrates how the unique set of contradictions and circumstances facing family farmers during the early twentieth century, including class exploitation, was connected to concern for their ability to serve the needs of U.S. industrial capitalist development. The argument presented here highlights the significant costs associated with the intensification of exploitation in the transition to industrial agriculture in the U.S. When viewed through the lens of class, the hallowed family farm becomes an example of one of the most exploitative institutions in the U.S. economy.

This book is suitable for students who study economic history, agricultural studies, and labor economics.

Elizabeth A. Ramey is Assistant Professor of Economics, Hobart and William Smith Colleges, USA.

New political economy
Richard McIntyre, General Editor

Class, Gender, and the American Family Farm in the 20th Century

Elizabeth A. Ramey

Routledge
Taylor & Francis Group

LONDON AND NEW YORK

First published 2014
by Routledge
2 Park Square, Milton Park, Abingdon, Oxon OX14 4RN

and by Routledge
711 Third Avenue, New York, NY 10017

Routledge is an imprint of the Taylor & Francis Group, an informa business

© 2014 Elizabeth A. Ramey

British Library Cataloguing in Publication Data
A catalogue record for this book is available from the British Library

Library of Congress Cataloging in Publication Data
Ramey, Elizabeth A.
Class, gender and the American family farm in the 20th century /
Elizabeth A. Ramey.
  pages cm
  1. Rural families–United States–Social conditions–20th century.
  2. Family farms–United States–History–20th century. I. Title.
  HD1476.U5R36 2014
  305.9'6309730904–dc23

                                                                2013039821

ISBN: 978-0-415-83472-8 (hbk)
ISBN: 978-1-315-79612-3 (ebk)

Typeset in Times New Roman
by Wearset Ltd, Boldon, Tyne and Wear

To my grandmother

Contents

x *Contents*

Figures

Tables

Acknowledgments

This book has been the overdetermined result of the wisdom, guidance, faith, and friendship of countless individuals and I want to thank all the teachers, colleagues, and friends who have contributed. This book would have never been possible without the insight and support of my faculty advisors at the University of Massachusetts, Richard Wolff, Stephen Resnick, Gerald Friedman, and Laura Lovett. My long and challenging journey toward achieving my professional goals has benefitted in so many ways from their example and advice. Rick and Steve have been my intellectual inspirations since I arrived at UMass, and will always be my teachers and role models. I will be forever grateful for their patience and confidence in me. I am grateful to Jerry for always finding the time to offer helpful advice, to push me forward, and in the process, to become my friend. I am forever indebted to Laura for guiding me to the treasure trove of research that informs this work, as well as to the community of scholars responsible for it.

This project could never have been completed without the support of Hobart and William Smith Colleges. Provosts Teresa Amott, Patrick McGuire, and Titilayo Ufomata generously provided funding to support my research. Dan Mulvey spent countless hours fulfilling my every request for library materials. Stan Weaver provided invaluable assistance with digital material. I am grateful for the work of my research assistants, Emily Davidowitz and Michael Fields, who cheerfully served at my beck and call. Last but certainly not least, I thank my colleagues in the Department of Economics for their constant mentorship and encouragement. The Department of Economics at the University of Denver provided space and support during my sabbatical leave while I worked on this manuscript. The Political Economy Research Institute (PERI) of Amherst, Massachusetts provided a dissertation fellowship to support my work.

Many other communities of scholars and friends have supported me in so many ways. Richard McIntyre provided an enthusiastic and helpful review. Without his support, the manuscript would not have found its home at Routledge. I am deeply indebted to George DeMartino and Ilene Grabel, two of the most incredible people I have ever met, who not only provide me with a magical, productive home-away-from-home, but also wisdom, guidance, friendship, and the courage to believe in myself. Max Fraad Wolff was there at the beginning, and has been a continual source of creative insights. I am eternally grateful for the intellectual "comraderie" I have found in the members of AESA. Their work has provided a condition of existence for my own. The ladies from my dissertation support group at the University of Massachusetts, Babette Faehmel and Liane Jeschull, have provided me with invaluable support for this project and for life in general. Many thanks as well to my writing coach, Gina Hiatt, and the members of my writing group for teaching me how to write through almost anything and seeing me through to the end. Jo Beth Mertens, Judith McKinney, and Leah Shafer have been my role models and friends, and have helped me to survive the first years on the tenure track. Brian Cooper, the "cat's meow," has provided humor and compassion at just the right moments. Judy Mahoney and Kathy Blanchard provided space to clear my head. Thank you, Bernie Gee, for dragging me across the finish line the first time. I am grateful to my aunt, Nancy Straub, who located and graciously provided access to our family photos, and who helped recover the stories behind them. Adam Reed provided faith, forgiveness, and so much more. To my dear friends, Gül Ünal and Chiara Piovani, I couldn't have done it without you. I am eternally grateful to my oldest friends, Mary Ann Hafer, Carolyn Smith and fellow farmer's daughter Kate Robey, for helping me to remember who I was, and for reminding me who I always wanted to be. Finally, I thank my grandmother, the "original" farmer's daughter, to whom I dedicate this work.

1   Introduction

This book develops and deploys a class analytical framework to examine the situation of family farms in the Midwestern United States during the early decades of the twentieth century. This new way of understanding the family farm constitutes the overall contribution of this project and yields a number of important results. First, I re-conceptualize the particular, crucial importance of women's roles in the contradictory conditions of U.S. agriculture at the time being investigated. Second, I recast the competitive struggle among corn farmers, state policy, and the trajectory of U.S. agriculture development in class terms. Third, I show how the unique set of contradictions and circumstances facing family farmers at this time, including class exploitation, had profound implications for the subsequent development, not only of U.S. agriculture, but of U.S. capitalism as well.

This first chapter is organized as follows: I first outline the theoretical framework which will be developed and deployed in further detail in the next chapter. I develop the framework using an analogy between the family farm and the medieval European manor. I then describe the historical context for the study of Midwestern farms from 1900–1930 by examining how the "farm woman problem" came to national attention during this time. I explain how farm women's descriptions of the problem can be understood in terms of class and the struggle over surplus labor. I conclude the historical overview with a discussion of how the farm woman problem, and farm women's work in general, played a role in the technological revolution that would transform American agriculture across the twentieth century, and how this transformation would enable the development of U.S. capitalism in a way that it would not have otherwise done. The final section of the chapter outlines the plan for the rest of the book.

Manor economy: a class analytical framework of the family farm

U.S. agriculture has historically displayed a rich variety of organizational forms. These have included, for example, the communal village plots of some Native American communities, the feudal Dutch patroonships along the Hudson River Valley in the Colonial period, the slave plantations of the South until the Civil War, the complex sharecropping system that grew to replace slavery, as well as the massive capitalist ranches that dotted the Western prairie across the late nineteenth century. One enduring organizational form has been that of the family farm, often touted as a uniquely American form of agricultural organization. Culturally iconic and politically influential, the family farm remains a mainstay of U.S. agriculture. The United States Department of Agriculture (USDA), for example, reports that 98 percent of farms in the United States are family farms (Hoppe and Banker 2010, i). The USDA defines a family farm as one in which the majority ownership and control of the business resides with a group of related individuals (Ahearn and Weber 2010).

What is a family farm? Answering this question is no simple matter. In fact, it is the work of this book to do so. Different theories generate different definitions of, or "truths" about, their basic concepts, even when those concepts share the same name. Deploying these uniquely defined concepts, each theory constructs its own conceptual world, and generates its own particular and partial explanations of that world. Different theories, or ways of thinking, therefore carry different implications and influence us to act differently in the worlds they show us (Wolff and Resnick 1987). For example, while the USDA develops and deploys its particular definition of the family farm and finds that it remains a ubiquitous organizational form in U.S. agriculture, others using different definitions of something called the family farm may and do come to very different conclusions about its existence and survival today. Thus, these competing definitions of "family farm" generate competing understandings of whether and how it needs saving, and therefore lead to very different policy prescriptions. In fact, with even a casual appraisal of popular press coverage of news and debates regarding U.S. agriculture, it is clear that the conceptual object, "family farm," is one that is highly contested.

This book develops its own unique understanding of the conceptual object called the "family farm." This is the first analysis to delineate and describe this particular object in terms of its constituent class processes and to examine the role of class in shaping the development of U.S. agriculture. No other researcher has yet applied this kind of class analysis to this particular conceptual object. In doing so, this analysis renders visible that which was previously invisible in other explanations of the family farm, with the goal of generating unique insights into its complexity, its crises, and its transformations during the time period under consideration.

The concept of class used and developed in this analysis is not a noun as in "working class" or "middle class," but an adjective describing the processes of production, appropriation, and distribution of surplus, or class processes. The surplus-based notion of class is one that Marx developed and systematically applied, particularly throughout the three volumes of his most developed work on his theory of the capitalist economy, *Capital*. This current book follows the body of work developed by Resnick and Wolff (1989) and others in this tradition which aims to provide a fuller formulation of Marx's surplus-based definition of class, and to apply it in various ways. I both draw upon and contribute to that body of work in deploying the class analytic framework toward an understanding of the family farm and its constituent class processes. That theoretical framework is introduced below. Detailed theoretical and empirical exposition of the family farm's class structures is presented in subsequent chapters.

In all societies, some individuals perform both necessary and surplus labor. Necessary labor is that which workers perform in order to produce the goods and services which society deems necessary for sustaining their labor as workers. Surplus is produced whenever workers produce goods and services above and beyond what is necessary. This surplus may be retained by the workers themselves, individually or collectively, or appropriated by others and distributed to still others. Whenever the surplus is appropriated and distributed by someone other than its direct producer, the class process is understood to be exploitative. Distributions of surplus are often required to secure the various natural, economic, political, and cultural conditions that constitute the class process, its conditions of existence. The fundamental class process involves the production and appropriation of surplus, while the subsumed class process refers to its distribution and receipt. Individuals may occupy, or personify, one or more positions in the fundamental or subsumed classes – as producer, appropriator/distributor, or recipient of surplus – or none at all. A class analysis, then, is one which examines the social organization of the surplus, as well as the impacts and conditions of existence of that particular organization (Resnick and Wolff 1989).

The dialectic provides the means, or logic, through which these class structural relationships are analyzed. Each relationship in society is understood to be the combined and complex result of the unique social processes which constitute it. Each of these processes, in turn, is the complex fitting-together of all the other social processes, the effect of their combined interactions. As such, processes, relationships, and structures in society are mutually constituted and interdependent. Each is overdetermined, and each participates in overdetermining all others. This dialectical logic highlights the contradictory, complex, and ever-changing aspects of social entities. Overdetermination implies that each is pushed and pulled in contradictory directions by the infinity of social processes constituting it. Its existence in contradiction produces its chaotic and uneven movement, or social change (Resnick and Wolff 1989).

Marx theorized five kinds of fundamental class process: ancient, slave, feudal, capitalist, and communist. All but the communist class processes are understood to be exploitative in the sense that the communist class process is the only one in which surplus is produced and appropriated collectively and by the same group of people. While the slave, feudal, and capitalist class processes involve the exploitation of the direct producer(s) by the first recipient(s) of surplus labor, the ancient class process involves auto, or self-exploitation. See Gabriel (1989) for a detailed discussion of exploitation and the ancient class process. See Hindess and Hirst (1975), and Resnick and Wolff (1989, 117–118) for discussion of the different kinds of class structures.

The different kinds of class processes have coexisted in varying combinations throughout history. For example, while the feudal class process was prevalent in the manorial economy of Western Europe from the twelfth through the early eighteenth centuries, hence lending its name to the period, feudal class processes have existed in other times and places. For example, Kayatekin (1990; 1996; 2001) locates feudal class processes in sharecropping arrangements in the post-bellum South, while Fraad et al. (1994) find a type of gender-based feudalism inside contemporary U.S. households. Likewise, other forms of class processes coexisted alongside the feudal in the manorial economy, as discussed below. The same can be said of any historical period, including the predominantly capitalist societies that have prevailed in the West since the transition from feudalism. Each kind of fundamental class process is constituted in particular times and places by unique conditions of existence which produce its particular qualities. The existence of different kinds of class processes alongside the dominant form may or may not signal the conditions for a transition to a new dominant form. Non-capitalist class processes such as the ancient and feudal may persist inside a predominantly capitalist society, for example, and even provide conditions of existence for the expansion of capitalism, and vice versa, without necessarily being in transition to capitalist forms themselves (Resnick and Wolff 1979; Gabriel 1990).

The family farm will be specified as a hybrid of different kinds of class structures − feudal, ancient, and capitalist. I focus in particular on the ancient and feudal class processes. In doing so, I build on the work of others who have located, elaborated, and extended Marx's analysis of these non-capitalist class structures, especially Gabriel (1989, 1990) on the ancient, and Kayatekin (1990; 1996; 2001) on the feudal class process; Fraad et al. (1994) on feudal households; and Resnick and Wolff (2009) on the interactions between feudal households and other class processes.

Marx focused his own work on the capitalist class structure, and secondarily on the non-capitalist forms, often insofar as he viewed them as "anti-conditions" for the development of capitalism (Gabriel 1990). A capitalist class process is one in which occupants of the fundamental class process are wage laborers and capitalists. Wage workers produce, and capitalist employers appropriate and distribute surplus value. The exploitation of workers is hidden in the wage labor relationship, which appears to be an equal exchange, but is actually the means through which capitalists appropriate the unpaid labor of their workers in the form of surplus value. Like the capitalist, the feudal class structure is exploitative in the sense that surplus labor is produced by someone other than its appropriator. Instead of being tied together through the market exchange involved in the wage labor relationship, however, the exploiter and exploited, or lord and serf, in a feudal class process are bound together by means of personal relations such as loyalty, obligation, tradition, affection, and/or force. In the case of gender-based household feudalism, lord and serf may be tied together through personal bonds of marriage, supported by gender ideologies defining appropriate roles for men and women in such a relationship (Fraad et al. 1994). Such personal ties may also serve to obscure the exploitative relationship between lord and serf. Finally, the ancient class process is marked by a lone, independent producer, appropriator, and distributor. The ancient is sometimes referred to in related terms such as "small producer," "artisan," "independent craftsman," "petty producer," or "self-employed." As the sole appropriator and distributor, the ancient is self-exploiting in the sense that even though she retains the fruits of her own labor on an individualized basis, she is nevertheless alienated from other direct producers in the acts of private, rather than communal, production and appropriation. The ancient's self-exploitation may be enabled and obscured by "selfist" ideologies that celebrate the individual self, independence, and autonomy (Gabriel 1990).

Kenneth Levin's 2004 work on the concept of class structural hybrids provides the foundation for the specification of the family farm as a hybrid. Based on his reading of various passages in Marx's works, he defines a hybrid as a combination of "different kinds of class structures at the same site" (Levin 2004, 5). He further defines a concept of "primitive hybrid" as one that combines "different forms of the same kind of class structure" rather than different kinds of class structure (Levin 2004, 29). Although Levin concentrates his investigation on hybrid class structures involving only two kinds of class structure – capitalist and one other – he includes the possibility of multiple kinds of class structures combining in one site (Levin 2004, 6). I apply the conceptual framework to investigate this possibility, and add the coexistence of different forms of hybrids in the same site, the family farm, or what may be called a hybrid of hybrids.

This follows on from the way in which I conceptualize the class structural hybrid that constitutes the family farm as containing two linked but distinct locations: the farm enterprise and the farm household. The family farm is a composite of its household, where members of the farm family are produced and reproduced, and its enterprise, where farm products and livestock are produced and reproduced. Both the farm household and the farm enterprise will be shown to be the site of one or more forms or kinds of the class processes contained in a family farm, but they typically do not contain the same forms or kinds of class processes. Because of this, I conceptualize them as distinct locations within the family farm, and as distinct manifestations of hybrids.

The manor economy of medieval Europe provides an analogy to illustrate the unique class taxonomy of the family farm that I develop and apply in this book. The manor typically included a feudal class structure in which serfs, linked to lords through ties of personal devotion and dependence, performed surplus labor on the lord's demesne.[1] Through the system of corvèe (which literally means "demand" or "requisition"), lords appropriated the surplus labor of their serfs who labored in the lord's fields, meadows, and stables, as well as in his household, workshop, mills, woods, etc. The demesne labor force also included wage laborers, who were employed to work in the fields, especially at harvest time, or for other tasks that were not covered by the customary services owed by the serfs. Household servants were retained as wage laborers as well. Sometimes the serfs themselves also kept serfs or employed wage workers in their households as servants, or to perform the labor services owed to their lords in their stead. Finally, the manor included self-employed artisans working as carpenters, butchers, bakers, brewers, coopers, tanners, and others in similar "by-employments."

Ancients sometimes worked in the demesne fields repairing fences and other structures, for example. In addition, the lord employed ancients as tutors, midwives, healers, and entertainers in his household.[2]

Consequently, the manor, like a family farm, was a site of different class structures – feudal, ancient, and perhaps capitalist – occurring together. As such, the manor was the site of a feudal/ancient/capitalist class structural hybrid. These different kinds of class processes occurred in different spaces or locations within the same manor, including the lord's enterprise and the lord's household. The demesne enterprise and household displayed different forms of hybrids, as different kinds of class structures combined differently in the enterprise and the household. The enterprise was the site of mostly feudal, and only sometimes capitalist or ancient class processes, while the lord's household regularly combined feudal, ancient, and capitalist forms of surplus (Duby 1998).

Not only was the manor a complex hybrid of different kinds of class structure, individuals in the manor often personified the intersection of multiple class positions in interesting, and perhaps contradictory ways. In many instances, this intersection involved individuals occupying different positions in different fundamental class processes. Wealthier serfs, as mentioned above, often hired servants to work in their homes, or kept serfs of their own. In these situations they personified a capitalist or feudal exploiter. In performing surplus labor on the lord's demesne, however, they occupied the position of feudal exploited. A serf often also worked as an independent craftsman, therefore participating in an ancient fundamental class process, individually appropriating his own surplus labor, as well as being exploited in his labor for the lord.

The intersection of class processes might also have involved individuals occupying two or more positions in both fundamental and subsumed class processes. In England, for example, a reeve or grave was elected annually from among the serfs to supervise and manage the performance of labor services in the lord's agricultural enterprise. The serf/reeve therefore occupied both the position of exploited feudal serf, and also of feudal subsumed class manager, overseeing and enabling his own and others' continued feudal exploitation.

Like the medieval European manor, a typical family farm included a feudal class structure. This was displayed in a unique form in which a married woman and her children occupied class positions as serfs performing surplus labor for their lord-husband/father in both the farm household and the farm enterprise. In addition, the family farm sometimes included a possible capitalist class structure, as the farmer periodically employed hired hands to work in the fields. The husband was not only a feudal lord and possibly sometimes a capitalist, but he also labored on his own in farm production, performing and appropriating his own surplus labor as an ancient.

Also like the manor, a typical family farm displayed different forms of hybrids, or different combinations of class structures in its two locations. The household typically displayed different forms of the feudal class process. Most of the labor performed there was performed by the farm wife, and occurred together with the feudal class process. Older females and younger children of both genders were often required to help their mother, laboring alongside her possibly as her serfs, making a primitive hybrid of different forms of feudalism. Only in rare, special cases was hired help employed in the farm household.

In the farm enterprise, most of the labor performed in the farm fields most of the time occurred along with the ancient class process. Most of the labor performed in the barnyard and garden, and some of the labor in the farm fields, occurred with the feudal surplus labor of wife and children. Finally, some labor may have occurred there along with the capitalist class process. The presence of a market in labor power is one condition for the existence of a capitalist class process, but does not, in itself, necessarily imply it. Various other economic, political, and cultural conditions participate in producing a capitalist relationship between employer and wage laborer. It is unlikely that the labor of hired "girls" in the family farm household occurred in the context of a capitalist class process. On the other hand, many of the hired hands in the ancient farm enterprise were probably engaged in a capitalist class process. This may have occurred, for example, if the ancient family farmer was also a capitalist employer or, as Marx referred to him, a "small master" (Levin 2004). The various possibilities are discussed further in Chapter 2, but it seems likely that hired hands often labored in the context of capitalist class processes in commercial farm production.

Hence, while the typical family farm household was only feudal, the typical family farm enterprise was either a feudal/ancient, ancient/capitalist, or feudal/ancient/capitalist class structural hybrid.

Figure 1.1 illustrates the class taxonomy of the typical family farm as described above. The family farm is comprised of its two locations, the farm household and the farm enterprise. Each location contains one or more kinds of

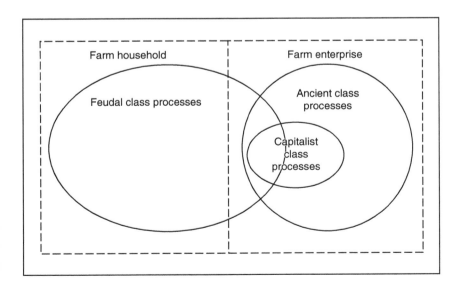

Figure 1.1 A typical family farm.

class processes. The feudal class structure of the family farm occurs in both locations, either by itself, or in conjunction with other class structures. It occurs by itself when the farm wife labors alone or with her children in the household, barnyard, or garden. It occurs in conjunction with other class structures when the farm wife and children labor alongside the farm husband, and sometimes hired farm workers, in the farm fields. As shown, the farm household is only feudal, while the farm enterprise is a hybrid of different kinds of class structures.

The labor of the ancient farmer in the family farm enterprise was most often directed toward the production of commercial crops, or means of production, such as fodder for these crops, while the labor of the feudal farm wife (unless she was helping the ancient farmer) was most often directed toward the production of farm produce, or the proceeds of these, for the use of the farm family. I therefore refer to, for example, the "ancient farm enterprise," the "ancient commercial farm enterprise," the "ancient/feudal hybrid commercial farm enterprise," or the "mostly-ancient hybrid commercial farm enterprise" to distinguish the former portion of the family farm enterprise, and to the "feudal farm enterprise" to distinguish the latter. Likewise, I refer to "ancient farm production," "ancient commercial farm production," "ancient/feudal farm production," or "mostly-ancient farm production" to distinguish the former kinds of labor processes, and to "feudal farm production" to distinguish the latter.

Like individual manor occupants, farm family members navigated multiple, and sometimes conflicting, class processes and positions. A farmer/husband was feudal, ancient, and sometimes possibly capitalist appropriator. As such, he faced the complexity of securing conditions of existence for up to three different fundamental class processes through distributions of his appropriated surplus. A farm wife might have occupied the position of feudal serf in relation to her farmer/husband, while acting as feudal lord in relation to her own children, thereby having to cope with potentially conflicting roles as both mother and exploiter. A farm wife might have occupied the position of feudal serf in the production of household goods and services, while occupying the position of ancient subsumed class manager in her capacity as keeper of commercial farm accounts, a situation that many farm women experienced (and still do). She might, therefore, have been exploited in one capacity, while at the same time holding some command over value flows as farm manager, and in this capacity enabling her husband's freedom from exploitation by others (or in other words, his self-exploitation as an ancient). If she also managed household accounts, she would also, like the English reeve, have been feudal serf, as well as subsumed class enabler of her own, and possibly her children's, exploitation by participating in securing the conditions of existence for the family farm's feudal class structure.

The family farm was, thus, a hybrid of class structures and their associated revenues and expenditures. Family farm class revenues stemmed from the performance and appropriation of ancient, capitalist, and feudal surplus labor. Recall that the ancient and capitalist class structures most often occurred only in the family farm enterprise, along with the labor of the farmer/husband, while the feudal class structure occurred in both the farm enterprise and the farm household along with the labor of the farm wife and children in both farm and household production. To secure its necessary conditions of existence, each of the three kinds of class structure required that expenditures, or subsumed class payments, be distributed from that surplus in various forms and to various recipients inside and outside the family farm. In addition to class revenues, the family farm may also have received non-class revenues and made various expenditures to ensure their continued receipt. Such revenues and distributions may have arisen from the transfer of value between the different kinds of class structures within the same family farm. Alternatively, they may have arisen from the transfer of value between the same kinds of class structures between family farms, or between different kinds of class structures between family farms and non-farm enterprises or government. Chapter 2 focuses on the former: It examines the patterns of non-market interaction among farm family members and workers shaping, and shaped by, these value transfers. Chapter 3 presents an analogous analysis of the latter – it examines the patterns of market interaction and competition among farmers shaping and shaped by these value transfers (called super profits), and between farmers and non-farm agribusinesses or governments.[3]

The class structural complexity of the family farm has significant implications, as it contributes to explaining its constant existence in crisis, at the same time as it sheds light on its tenacity and the particular and crucial adaptations it has made to survive. The several kinds of class structure occurring in different combinations in different locations on the family farm create multiple opportunities for class crisis to occur. If conditions of existence are not secured for any one of these class processes, the family farm may suffer from crisis. However, just as crisis points are multiplied, class structural complexity increases the flexibility to generate resolutions to these crises. Surplus produced and appropriated in one kind of class structure can be transferred to another kind of class structure and between sites of production to help secure threatened conditions of existence as needs arise. For example, revenues from the sale of hybrid produce could be used to support feudal class structures in the farm household. Likewise, revenues from feudal farm produce could be used to support feudal class structures in the farm household, or transferred to the ancient class structures in the farm enterprise. Which of these strategies family farmers employed to resolve the crisis they faced during the early twentieth century, and with what contradictory consequences, will be a focal point of this analysis. Family farm production as a whole will be shown to depend on the coexistence of its different kinds of class structures, even as those class structures shrink and expand in response to crisis and prosperity at various times and under various circumstances. Despite dramatic changes in these class processes and their conditions of existence, the family farm has continued to survive and, in many cases, to flourish.

For a variety of complex reasons, discussed further in Chapter 2, the ancient class structure took priority for most family farms. Even though it was but one among the different kinds of class structures occurring there, the ancient class process was widely considered to be the heart, or essence, of the family farm, and it was for that which its members toiled and sacrificed. Ancient farmers were not likely to be able to appropriate enough surplus from their own labor to sustain and reproduce themselves as ancients. Even if they were, the limitations of self-exploitation rendered them less able to respond and adapt to changed conditions of existence. In his groundbreaking work on the theory of ancients, Gabriel identified the limitations of the ancient producer thus:

> It is not possible for the ancient producer to obtain more necessary and/or surplus labor than the total labor she performs. This may be a problem that is unique to the ancient producer, in the sense that the only source of additional wealth or of reduced production costs within the ancient fundamental class process is the labor of the appropriator.
>
> (Gabriel 1989, 171–172)

Feudal and capitalist workers changed the picture. They could be enlisted to provide more surplus labor, to help reduce costs of production, or both. Family farm members adjusted all of the farm's revenues and expenditures so as to maximize net outlays for the ancient class structure – the essence and the "real" business of the family farm. The primacy of the ancient class structure in the family farm hybrid, coupled with its limitations, combined to create the conditions for its continued existence, so that the family farm hybrid has not been a temporary, transitional form.

In the next chapter, I will focus on the implications of the reconceptualization of farm women's (and children's) importance in the family farm as feudal serfs laboring in both the farm household and the farm enterprise. It was the family farm's feudal class structure that was an important source of subsidies to the ancient class structure of the farm enterprise. These subsidies came in the form of the feudal surplus labor of wives and children working in the fields, tending livestock, and growing farm produce. The feudal surplus labor of farm wives also enabled a reduced necessary labor in farm production since the ancient farmer's consumption (as well as that of his workers) derived from the household feudal surplus labor appropriated from his wife. This subsidized consumption allowed the farmer to appropriate a large proportion – perhaps all – of his labor as surplus, and distribute it toward the survival of the ancient farm enterprise. In this way, the hybrid class structure of the family farm enabled the ancient farmer to transcend the limits of the ancient class structure, constrained as it is by the lone producer of surplus, and pushed the boundaries of necessary labor toward zero. At the same time, this arrangement required an increasingly insupportable rate of feudal exploitation in family farms, contributing to a crisis for U.S. agriculture. That crisis took the form of "the farm woman problem."

Class struggle on the farm: constructing the "farm woman problem"

Midwestern farmers enjoyed unprecedented prosperity during the first two decades of the twentieth century. As Secretary of Agriculture Wilson noted happily in his fourteenth annual report in 1910, "Year after year it has been my privilege to record another most prosperous year in agriculture" (USDA 1910). Secretary Wilson's enthusiasm was not unjustified; 1910 marked the thirteenth year of recovery from a downturn in 1897 and the beginning of what would become the Golden Age of high and stable prices from 1910–1914. The good times would continue unabated through World War I, until demand and prices sagged in the summer of 1920.

Yet, progressive reformers grew increasingly concerned with the "backwardness" of agriculture – a lack of sufficient economic, social, and cultural progress – that ostensibly threatened not only rural, but national well-being. For a nation in the throes of industrialization and urbanization, farm prosperity presented a paradox. Prices were high and stable because production was not keeping pace with population and export growth. For urban consumers of both food and labor power – workers and capitalists – the Golden Age raised fears of Malthusian style food crises and instability. Workers' access to cheap and plentiful food was an important factor in keeping wages low and profits high while maintaining (or in the case of falling food prices, even increasing) workers' standards of living. Cheap and plentiful food was a lynchpin of U.S. economic development because it enabled continually intensifying rates of exploitation of workers, offset by rising consumption. Together, these would finance the combination of economic growth and domestic stability that would become a foundation for the United States' global dominance (Resnick and Wolff 2006). Spurred on by these concerns, President Theodore Roosevelt appointed the Country Life Commission to study the problems of rural life in 1908. In his letter of appointment to the Commission's chair, Cornell Professor Liberty Hyde Bailey, he explained his motivations thus:

> There is but one person whose welfare is as vital to the welfare of the whole country as is that of the wage-worker who does manual labor; and that is the tiller of the soil the farmer – for it is upon their welfare, material and moral, that the welfare of the rest of the nation ultimately rests.
>
> (Roosevelt 1908)

The dynamics of class struggle between capitalists and workers, and their joint interest in access to cheap food pitted them against farmers, helped promote the issue of rural progress to the forefront of national attention, and shaped the construction of "the farm woman problem." The Country Life Commission grew into the Country Life Movement, a coalition of young intellectuals including rural journalists, editors of farm journals, and educators (including agricultural college professors), along with some urban businessmen with an interest in rural prosperity, government agricultural officials, leaders of rural organizations, and urban do-gooders. The Country Life reformers sought to bring American Progressivism to the farm (Bowers 1971, 212). One of their primary goals was to promote the application of scientific methods and the use of mechanized equipment in farming. This "New Agriculture" would increase efficiency, ensuring that farmers could still produce enough food to feed the growing population – even as their own numbers declined (Jellison 1993, 4).

Fears of an impending scarcity of food were linked to the perception of rural flight, as well as to the problem of flagging productivity growth. The vision of the New Agriculture relied on a population of farmers who were prosperous and stable enough to afford the new equipment, and educated enough to be able to use it effectively. Rural depopulation threatened to drain the countryside of the required people and resources. As a Michigan farm woman wrote in 1915, "The rural community is robbed of its most helpful influences by the constant exodus from the country of its brightest boys and girls" (USDA 1915, 26). Advertisers, journalists, and policymakers directed their attention to the pressing question: "How we gonna keep 'em down on the farm?" (Kleinegger 1988; Neth 1998)

A second primary goal of the Country Life movement was to address this question by promoting "rural uplift," to "make the social, intellectual, and economic aspects of country life more satisfying" (Bowers 1971, 211). The New Agriculture, with its focus on mechanization and rationalization of farm production, meant that farm labor requirements would decline, freeing family members, especially farm women, to focus on this "rural uplift" component of the Country Life agenda. As the keepers of hearth and home envisioned by reformers, who sought to promote the urban homemaker ideal in the countryside, women instead of men would "naturally" have responsibility for these tasks. The problem was that young farm women were leading the charge to the city.

In 1913, the prominent Country Life reformer, Herbert Quick, labeled the rural flight problem "largely a woman movement" in an article that appeared in *Good Housekeeping* magazine (Jellison 1993, 5). Decades before the mass extinction of farms grabbed national attention following World War II, farmers' daughters led the exodus from rural areas. Consistently rising male to female population ratios in the rural Midwest attest to the scarcity of women in rural areas (Banks and Beale 1973; Jellison 1993). In an article entitled "Why Young Women are Leaving Our Farms," the *Literary Digest* traced the problem to the long hours of work, the isolation, and the drudgery of farm life for many Midwestern women. "Becoming a trifled bored with this unexciting round of toil," the author explained, "the farmer's daughter casts an understanding eye at the neighboring farmer's son who has been hanging around her ivy-clad porch, reflects upon what he has to offer, and catches the next train to Squedunk or New York" (1920). Henry Wallace, a member of the Country Life Commission and editor of the widely read *Wallace's Farmer*, opined in a 1914 editorial, "Until we make life on the farm satisfying to the farmer's wife, we will labor in vain to check the drift of rural population to the towns and cities" (Jellison 1993, 5).

The question of rural flight had another dimension, related to the influence of eugenics, to which a few prominent Progressives, including Theodore Roosevelt, subscribed. As the "brightest boys and girls" departed for the greater convenience and opportunities of city life, reformers feared that those left behind would be of "inferior" quality. The influx of immigrants, mostly from southern and eastern Europe, both to overcrowded cities and to depopulating rural areas, spurred these concerns. Adhering to a form of agrarian mythology, Country Life reformers contrasted these immigrants, who they characterized as "illiterate, docile, lacking in self-reliance and initiative" and their "peasant agriculture" with their own idealized version of the independent, progressive, hard-working yeoman farmers of northern European descent, who they viewed as the backbone of the nation (Bowers 1971, 217). They looked to the (white, northern European, middle class) farm family and rural life as the quintessential American institution and experience – a bulwark of "American" virtues and values against the onslaught of "foreign" ideas and people.

This aspect of the Country Life agenda served the interests of urban capitalists as well. Here, the concern was with maintaining a steady supply of cheap, well-disciplined, and reliable workers. The notion of "child crops" expresses this notion, and the importance of rural areas in supplying the necessary workforce to feed growing industry. Arguing for the importance of funding "rural uplift" for the health of the whole nation, reformer Mary Meek Atkeson made these connections explicit:

> In payment for this interest shown by the city people the farm will return not only its corn and hogs and cattle, but also a steady stream of bright-eyed young people to carry the best American traditions into every city in the land. As the farmer will tell you jokingly, his young folks are indeed the "best crop" of his farm.
>
> (Kline 2002, 91)

As farm women were key producers of this "child crop," the eugenics component further highlighted farm women's role in the Country Life agenda, and contributed to their view of "the farm women problem."

The Country Life Commission delivered its report in 1909, and pointed to the farm woman as a prime suspect in rural problems. "Whatever general hardships, such as poverty, isolation, and lack of labor-saving devices, may exist on any given farm, the burden of these hardships falls more heavily on the farmer's wife than on the farmer himself" (Country Life Commission 1917, 104). The overworked farm woman took center stage and the success of farm life – and therefore of the nation as a whole – was seen to rest on her tired shoulders.

The Commission's report sparked a flurry of surveys, reports, and articles on "the farm woman problem" (see Table 1.1). The white, middle-class farm women at whom reformers' efforts were aimed were a highly literate group, and they took these opportunities to express their concerns. *The Ladies' Home Journal* published excerpts from hundreds of letters from one of the earliest surveys by Mattie Corson, a farm woman whose mother had died of overwork. One woman wrote that she "would rather take my chances with my girl on

Broadway ... than to have her walk the sure road to the county asylum that I am heading for" (*The Ladies' Home Journal* 1909).[4] Martha Bensely Bruère and Robert Bruère described the "Revolt of the Farmer's Wife" in a series of articles published in *Harper's Bazaar* in 1912. They summed up the situation, thus: "Shall the nation go hungry because the farmers' wives don't like their jobs?" they asked. And then, "For, after all, a man will not live on the farm without a wife" (Bruère and Bruère 1912, 539).

In fact, if a man would not live on a farm without a wife, a woman could not, with rare exceptions, live on a farm without a husband. Women seldom had access to farming at all except as farmers' wives, or future farmers' mothers. On rare occasions they were "lady" farmers, but never just "farmers." *His* job was to be the farmer; *hers* was to make life bearable for him. Making life bearable, however, was becoming an almost unbearable burden for many farm women. Farm women and their advocates described their struggle with long hours of work, with isolation, and with a lack of proper equipment.

Intolerable working conditions were only part of the problem. Farm women struggled with their situation of dependency, drudgery, subordination, and undervaluation of their labor. Attention to the "farm woman problem" gave farm women and their daughters the opportunity to not just protest against their working and living conditions (as reformers had hoped), but also to express a much deeper injustice – that of the exploitative system that relied upon and reproduced the inequalities which relegated them and their work to secondary status, in spite of the value of their contributions to the survival of farm families and family farms. The class blindness of U.S. culture meant that farm women could criticize their circumstances in terms of the absence of equality, justice, and democracy but never in terms of class, and largely they did not recognize the role of class in their situations. Nevertheless, I argue that class did in fact play a significant role in explaining farm women's situations and in understanding the failure to address and resolve it.

Adding this class dimension to the analysis constitutes an intervention in the debate among feminist economic historians about whether or not changed work processes or access to new technologies was "liberating" for farm women or not (examples include Fink 1992, Jellison 1993, and Neth 1998). In fact, these things had contradictory impacts, overdetermined as they were by the process of class, a factor which is largely unrecognized in these discussions much as it was unrecognized in the discussions about the farm woman problem of the time.

Marx identified what was, for him, "the principal and as yet invisible violence of capitalism" in "the existence of a hidden flow of labor" (taking the form of "surplus value") from the worker to the capitalist (Gibson-Graham et al. 2001, 7). In the process of constructing and addressing the problems of rural life, reformers recovered a similar "invisible violence" occurring on family farms – that of class exploitation. Instead of occurring in the context of a wage relation, between capitalists and workers, this type of exploitation was occurring in the context of a marriage relation, between farmers and their wives. One set of class struggles – between capitalists and their workers – brought another to the surface. Lacking the language of class, farm women never explicitly identified their problems as associated with class exploitation – with the division of their workday between necessary and surplus labor, and with the desire to appropriate the fruits of their own labor. Yet many of them made clear that resolving "the farm woman problem" required something more than access to running water and an electric washing machine.

In 1913, Secretary of Agriculture David F. Houston solicited feedback from the wives of the USDA's 55,000 volunteer crop correspondents. Based on the 2,241 replies, the USDA began publishing a summary and series of four pamphlets in 1915. The *New York Times* published excerpts of the letters in a May 1915 article entitled "Farm Women Find Life Hard." While official interpretations of the responses focused on the need for labor-saving devices and extension services for farm homemakers (as suggested by the Country Life agenda), a deeper dissatisfaction was expressed in many of the letters. "Women have an innate longing for appreciation and a feeling that they are partners in fact with their husbands and not looked upon as subordinates," wrote one Iowa farm woman. One from Missouri complained of the undervaluation of farm women's work. "[T]he men needed to be educated up, as so many men think women's work does not amount to much and consequently has no commercial valuation." A woman from Minnesota compared her life on the farm to a life in jail, and professed to prefer the captivity of the latter over that of the former. "I have always lived on a farm except the first five years of my marriage, and I think I might almost as soon have been in jail, because the work is so hard and is never done" (*The New York Times* 1915; USDA 1915).

Minnie Boyer Davis of Josie, Nebraska wrote to Secretary Houston in 1916 explaining that the responses "from women all over the country tell the story, not complaint of work or lack of conveniences, but of *unequal status*" (Jellison 1993, 19). In addition to raising her two children, cooking, cleaning, gardening, sewing, working in the fields, and cooking for hired hands, Davis also wrote regularly for farm periodicals. In a 1916 letter to the *Farm Journal*, she argued that "You cannot consider agriculture without women. In short, there isn't any." Nevertheless, farm women (and therefore agriculture in general) suffered from an "unfortunate condition" because

> there is no equal status of women with men; because in the farm life the woman, though she shares the drudgery, has no initiative; because, though she is a producer she is seldom a spender; because, though she is the main-stay of the home, her work and part are not held in respect, nor given the position they should have; because her life and that of her children is largely shaped by someone other than herself; because, in short, the farm is a sort of monarchy instead of a democracy.
>
> (Davis 1916)

In 1921, *The Nation* declared "Feminism on the Farm" when it published the "Nebraska Farm Women's Declaration of Independence" which called not only for labor saving devices for the home, but equality for the women's and men's spheres of work in the home and the farm. Their final demand? "Our share of the farm income" (*The Nation* 1921, 440).

Farm women expressed a deep sense of injustice about their circumstances, while at the same time noting the special advantages of rural living and farming as a way of life, even if these sentiments did not conform to their own direct experiences. "In spite of all our disadvantages, the farm is the best place to live and raise a family of healthy, happy boys and girls" wrote a North Dakota farm wife in response to Secretary Houston's survey (USDA 1915, 20). This ambivalence can be viewed as an expression of the contradictory circumstances shaping the exploitative class structures on family farms, of which the farm woman problem was an expression. Some women theorized their positions on family farms in ways that celebrated, excused, or justified these positions. One example of these contradictory experiences and interpretations lies in Mary E. Wilkins' story, "The Revolt of Mother" and its aftermath. The fictional account of a woman who moves her family into the newly-constructed barn in protest against the comfort provided to the animals and not to people on her farm first appeared in *Harper's New Monthly Magazine* in 1890 (Wilkins 1890, 553–61). Wilkins' story was widely read and performed in homes, schools, and public venues, and was extremely influential in shaping the debate about farm women's lives and the farm woman problem (Garvey 2009). Wilkins later recanted the story, explaining that a real life farm woman "would have lacked the nerve," the "imagination," and "would never have dreamed of putting herself ahead of the Jersey cows which meant good money" (Kleinegger 1988, 175). Her denial of the story seems only to have confirmed the conflict, and denied the possibility of revolt, but it nevertheless signifies the multiple and sometimes contradictory ways that farm women and others recognized and responded to their circumstances. This, in turn, reflects the multiple influences conditioning the existence of family farm class structures, and their contradictory impacts in both supporting and undermining those structures. Table 1.1 summarizes the above discussion of "the farm woman problem" as reflected in various publications of the period.

Conclusion and plan of work

The farm woman problem was itself an expression of the contradictions stemming from the unique hybrid of the family farm's class structures. Farm women's labor helped subsidize the cheap and abundant food for urban dwellers, as well as the survival and prosperity of the family farm. Yet, this survival was being purchased at the expense of the farm family. The onerous burden on farm women was reflected in the concern for their plight expressed by Country Life reformers. Even in the most prosperous of times for American farmers, "[t]he farmer was making a living, but out of the lives of his womankind – careful to the last degree of his cattle and his swine, but utterly careless of the human beings of his home" (*The Ladies' Home Journal* 1909). The resulting crisis and disintegration of the family farm feudal class structures, therefore, disabled the ability of ancient farmers to continue to serve capitalist industry.

The farm woman problem must be situated in this larger context of concern for what was viewed as a general problem of rural backwardness, and its potential negative impact on capitalist industrial development, as seen in the stagnant productivity growth and high agricultural prices during agriculture's Golden Age. The problem of rising food prices was "one of the most talked-about economic issues" of the time (Danbom 1979, 30). The family farm's hybrid of class structures both supported and undermined its ability to serve the needs of capitalist industry in providing the required workers, cheap and abundant food, and market for industrial goods. Attention to the farm woman problem was a reflection of the importance of the farm family and therefore of the farm household as a central institution in the success or failure of family farms and rural life. The farm woman problem, therefore, became a device through which the inadequacy of family farm production to serve an expanding industrial capitalism's needs could be discussed, investigated, and dealt with as either "solvable" within the framework of existing rural institutions, or else unsolvable in such a context, and therefore requiring the reorganization of rural society in general and of the family farm in particular.

The broad coalition of interests that formed the Country Life Movement coalesced around the recognition that a revolutionary reorganization of rural life was necessary. This would require thoroughgoing change in not only the family farm household, but also in the family farm enterprise – in both the feudal and the ancient class structures. Because discussion of the role of class processes and exploitation in generating the dilemma was never recognized, this agenda for radical restructuring did not, of course, include the transition toward non-exploitative class processes in family farms. Nor, for the most part, did the parameters of official "solutions" even aim to address the injustices that farm women did identify and struggled to challenge. If, as I argue, the farm woman problem was in fact overdetermined by the contradictions and limitations of exploitative feudal (and ancient) class processes in family farms, it was therefore never resolved. Instead, a central thrust of reform efforts was to promote the application of technology and scientific management practices to improve "efficiency" in the farm home, and especially in the farm enterprise.

In a sense, the answer to the limits of feudal exploitation, as well as the limits of ancient self-exploitation, became the first of the two major prongs of the Country Life agenda, that of technical change in commercial farm production. Internal subsidies from farm women and children were thereby supplemented by external subsidies from other farmers (through the hunt for super profits) and the state (through government farm programs). These processes of technical change in ancient farm production, and the associated ruthless competitive struggle among family farms shifted U.S. agriculture onto a new trajectory of development which fueled the rise of capitalist agribusiness at the same time that it produced a rural landscape increasingly littered with failed farms and crumbling communities, and hence the need for the state to supplement the subsidies from

Table 1.1 The "farm woman problem"

Title	Description	On farm women
"The Revolt of Mother" by Mary E. Wilkins, 1890	Mary E. Wilkins penned this story of a farm wife who moved her family into the new barn in protest of the disparate living conditions between human and beast on her farm. She later recanted the story, saying the real life farm women "would have lacked the nerve," "the imagination," and "would never have dreamed of putting herself ahead of Jersey cows which meant good money" (Kleinegger 1988, 175).	Her mother scrubbed a dish fiercely. "You ain't found out yet we're women-folks, Nanny Penn," said she. "You ain't seen enough of men-folks yet to. One of these days you'll find it out, an' then you'll know that we know only what men-folks think we do, so far as any use of it goes, an' how we'd ought to reckon men-folks in with Providence, an' not complain of what they do any more than we do of the weather."
Country Life Commission, 1909	7-member, all-male commission appointed by President Roosevelt to study the problems of rural life; stemming from Progressive concerns which linked urban stability to rural prosperity, scientific agriculture, and rural uplift. Inspired by the Commission's recommendations, the rural arm of American Progressivism, the Country Life Movement, emerged.	"Realizing that the success of country life depends in very large degree on the woman's part, the Commission has made special effort to ascertain the condition of women on the farm." "Report of the Commission on Country Life," January 1909 (Country Life Commission 1917).
Mattie Corson's Bachelor Girls' Club survey, 1909	Organized by Mattie Corson, a farm woman whose mother had died of overwork. A survey of "girls and women of marriageable age and over, single and married, in the country." The over 900 responses were excerpted in *Ladies Home Journal*.	"I would rather take my chances with my girl on Broadway, than to have her walk the sure road to the county asylum that I am heading for."

Source	Description	Quote
Martha Bensley Bruère and Robert Bruère's series of articles entitled "The Revolt of the Farmer's Wife" and "After the Revolt" in *Harper's Bazaar*, 1912	The Bruères raised several issues pertaining to the farm woman problem, and linked the issue explicitly to the problem of rising food prices for the rapidly increasing urban population.	"Shall the nation go hungry because the farmers' wives don't like their jobs? For, after all, a man will not live on the farm without a wife."
Secretary of Agriculture, David F. Houston's survey of the wives of USDA volunteer crop correspondents, 1913	Based on the 2,241 replies, the USDA began publishing a summary and series of four pamphlets in 1915. The *New York Times* covered the report in a May 30, 1915 article, "Farm Women Find Life Hard."	"I have always lived on a farm except the first five years of my marriage, and I think I might almost as soon have been in jail, because the work is so hard and is never done" (USDA, "Social and Labor Needs of Farm Women," 46).
The Farmer's Wife	Published 1896–1939 when it was absorbed by *Farm Journal*. With a circulation of 1.25 million, it was the most popular women's magazine for a rural audience.	
Nebraska Farm Women's Declaration of Independence, 1921	Published in an October 19th article "Feminism on the Farm" in *The Nation* magazine.	"Our Demands: A power washing-machine for the house for every tractor bought for the farm. A bath-tub in the house for every binder on the farm. Running water in the kitchen for every riding-plow for the fields. A kerosene cook-stove for every automobile truck. A fireless cooker for every new mowing-machine. Our share of the farm income."

farm women with its own massive subsidies to ancient farmers. This reorganization gradually replaced the complex model of general farming in place in the Midwest at the time with a different one of highly-specialized, ever larger, "factories in the fields." The limitations of the ancient/feudal hybrid of class structures in family farms were partially surmounted through increased productivity and state supports which shaped a hunt for super profits, resulting in an expanding mass and rate of surplus in family farming. This became the vehicle for "resolving" the problems of rural life and backward agriculture in terms of fuelling capitalist industrial development. Labor-saving technology in ancient commercial farm production "released" millions of farmers and workers from rural areas, created markets for industrial products for the farm enterprise and the farm home, and ensured a steady and abundant supply of cheap food. These successes would come at the expense of massive dislocation in the countryside as millions of family farms collapsed. One agricultural scientist, Eugene Davenport, explained this necessary march of progress in the interests of the greater good:

> The great laws of evolution and the survival of the fittest will continue to operate, and, in the interest of progress, they ought to operate. Progress is not in the interest of the individual, and it cannot stop because of individuals. Everything must surrender to the central idea that this is a movement for the highest attainable agriculture in the fullest possible sense of the term.
>
> (Danbom 1979, 40)

As this book shows, these developments were neither necessary nor necessarily "progressive" but rather the complex, contingent, overdetermined results of class struggle within and between family farms, and between family farms and the non-farm economy, as well as the non-class processes conditioning these struggles.

The remainder of the book is organized as follows: in Chapter 2, I present the detailed description of the family farm's ancient/feudal hybrid class structure. I focus on the transfers between the feudal and ancient class structures within the same family farm, and show how its survival has relied on a ruthless exploitation of farm women, children, and men in rural life. Chapter 3 adds to the analysis by examining the transfers between ancient class structures in different family farm enterprises, and between family farm enterprises and non-farm agribusiness and governments. I show how the survival of the family farm has been connected to a ruthless competition in which some farmers cannibalize others in a hunt for super profits, shaping technical change in ancient farm production, while non-farm agribusinesses thrive on the carnage. I develop a class analysis of state policies and how these provide a necessary supplement to the subsidies from the feudal to the ancient class structures within the family farm, whilst also serving to intensify the perpetual crisis that mainly benefits the few at the expense of the many. Chapter 4 presents a concluding summary of the main points of the book, as well as its significance.

Notes

1 The demesne is the portion of the manor retained by the lord for his own use. The remainder of the manor was let out to the serf tenants.
2 In certain time periods and locations, the manor labor force also included slaves, who performed the bulk of daily maintenance tasks, in the Lord's household, for example, rather than wage laborers (Duby 1998, 37).
3 The following equation represents the hybrid class structure of the family farm, and its revenues and expenditures in simple class terms:

$$SL(A) + SL(CAP) + SL(F) + NCR = SSCP(A) + SSCP(CAP) + SSCP(F) + Y$$

The first three terms on the left hand side designate the surplus labor produced and appropriated in the family farm's three kinds of class structures: ancient (A), capitalist (CAP), and feudal (F). The corresponding terms on the right hand side designate the subsumed class payments necessary to secure the conditions of existence for each of the three kinds of class structure. The NCR term stands for non-class revenues, and Y for whatever expenditures were required to ensure their continued receipt.
4 The belief that rural women were prone to insanity was so widespread that the USDA felt obliged to address the problem directly in its 1915 report on a survey of the wives of crop correspondents. Having found no evidence to support the charge "that farm women contribute largely to the inmates of asylums," the report authors explained that "statements to the effect that life on farms drives women insane have been omitted" USDA 1915, 24; Sachs 1983, 23).

References

Ahearn, Mary C., and Jeremy Weber. 2010. "Farm Household Economics and Well Being: Glossary." USDA Economic Research Service. November. Available online at www.ers.usda.gov/Briefing/WellBeing/.

Banks, Vera J., and Calvin L. Beale. 1973. "Farm Population Estimates 1910–70. Rural Development Service Statistical Bulletin No. 523." USDA Economic Research Service. Washington, DC

Bowers, William L. 1971. "Country-Life Reform, 1900–1920: A Neglected Aspect of Progressive Era History." *Agricultural History* 45 (3) (July 1): 211–221.

Bruère, Martha Bensley, and Robert Walter Bruère. 1912. "Revolt of the Farmer's Wife." *Harper's Bazaar*, March.

Country Life Commission. 1917. "Report of the Commission on Country Life." New York: Sturgis & Walton.

Danbom, David B. 1979. *The Resisted Revolution: Urban America and the Industrialization of Agriculture, 1900–1930*. Ames: Iowa State University Press.

Davis, Minnie Boyer. 1916. "Letter to the Editor." *Farm Journal*.

Duby, Georges. 1968. *Rural Economy and Country Life in the Medieval West*. Translated by Cynthia Postan. London: Edward Arnold.

Fraad, Harriet, Stephen Resnick, and Richard Wolff. 1994. *Bringing It All Back Home*. London and Boulder, CO: Pluto Press.

Fink, Deborah. 1992. *Agrarian Women: Wives and Mothers in Rural Nebraska, 1880–1940*. Studies in Rural Culture. Chapel Hill and London: University of North Carolina Press.

Gabriel, Satyananda. 1989. "Ancients: a Marxian Theory of Self-exploitation." PhD Dissertation. Amherst, MA: University of Massachusetts.

Gabriel, Satyananda. 1990. "Ancients: A Marxian Theory of Self-Exploitation." *Rethinking Marxism* 3 (1): 85–106.

Garvey, Ellen Gruber. 2009. "Less Work for 'Mother': Rural Readers, Farm Papers, and the Makeover of 'The Revolt of "Mother."'" *Legacy* 26 (1): 119–135.

Gibson-Graham, J. K., Stephen Resnick, and Richard Wolff. 2001. *Re/presenting Class: Essays in Postmodern Marxism*. Durham, NC and London: Duke University Press.

Hindess, Barry, and Paul Q. Hirst. 1975. *Pre-capitalist Modes of Production*. London: Routledge and Kegan Paul.

Hoppe, Robert A. and Banker, David E. 2010. "Structure and Finances of U.S. Farms: Family Farm Report, 2010 Edition." USDA Economic Research Service. Available online at www.ers.usda.gov/Publications/EIB24/.

Jellison, Katherine. 1993. *Entitled to Power*. Chapel Hill: University of North Carolina Press.

Kayatekin, Serap Ayşe. 1990. "A Class Analysis of Sharecropping." PhD Dissertation. Amherst, MA: University of Massachusetts.

Kayatekin, Serap Ayşe. 1996. "Sharecropping and Class: A Preliminary Analysis." *Rethinking Marxism* 9 (1) (March): 28–57.

Kayatekin, Serap Ayşe. 2001. "Sharecropping and Feudal Class Processes in the Postbellum Mississippi Delta." In *Re/presenting Class: Essays in Postmodern Marxism*, edited by J.K. Gibson-Graham, Stephen Resnick, and Richard Wolff. Durham, NC and London: Duke University Press.

Kleinegger, Christine. 1988. "Out of the Barns and into the Kitchens: Transformations in Farm Women's Work in the First Half of the Twentieth Century." In *Women, Work, and Technology: Transformations*, edited by Barbara Drygulski Wright. Ann Arbor: University of Michigan Press.

Kline, Ronald R. 2002. *Consumers in the Country: Technology and Social Change in Rural America*. Baltimore: The Johns Hopkins University Press.

Levin, Kenneth M. 2004. "Enterprise Hybrids and Alternative Growth Dynamics." PhD Dissertation. Amherst, MA: University of Massachusetts. Available online at http://scholarworks.umass.edu/dissertations/AAI3118314.

Neth, Mary C. 1998. *Preserving the Family Farm: Women, Community, and the Foundations of Agribusiness in the Midwest, 1900–1940*. Baltimore: The Johns Hopkins University Press.

Resnick, Stephen A., and Richard D. Wolff. 1979. "The Theory of Transitional Conjunctures and the Transition from Feudalism to Capitalism in Western Europe." *Review of Radical Political Economics* 11 (3): 3–22.

Resnick, Stephen A., and Richard D. Wolff. 1989. *Knowledge and Class: A Marxian Critique of Political Economy*. Chicago and London: University Of Chicago Press.

Resnick, Stephen A., and Richard D. Wolff. 2006. "Exploitation, Consumption, and the Uniqueness of U.S. Capitalism." In *New Departures in Marxian Theory*, by Stephen A. Resnick and Richard D. Wolff, 341–353. London and New York: Routledge.

Resnick, Stephen A., and Richard D. Wolff. 2009. "The Class Analysis of Households Extended: Children, Fathers, and Family Budgets." In *Class Struggle on the Home Front Work, Conflict, and Exploitation in the Household*, edited by Graham Cassano, 86–115. London and New York: Palgrave Macmillan.

Roosevelt, Theodore. 1908. "Letter to Professor Liberty Hyde Bailey Creating the Commission on Country Life", August 10. Available online at www.theodoreroosevelt.com/images/research/txtspeeches/299.txt.

Sachs, Carolyn. 1983. *The Invisible Farmers: Women in Agricultural Production.* Totowa, NJ: Rowman and Allanheld.

The Ladies' Home Journal. 1909. "Is This the Trouble With the Farmer's Wife?" February.

The Literary Digest. 1920. "Why Young Women Are Leaving Our Farms." October 2.

The Nation. 1921. "Feminism on the Farm." October 19.

The New York Times. 1915. "Farm Women Find Life Hard." May 30.

United States Department of Agriculture (USDA). 1910. "Report of the Secretary of Agriculture." Washington, DC: Government Printing Office.

United States Department of Agriculture (USDA). 1915. "Social and Labor Needs of Farm Women." Report 103. Washington, DC: Government Printing Office.

Wilkins, Mary E. 1890. "The Revolt of Mother." *Harper's New Monthly Magazine*, September.

Wolff, Richard D., and Stephen A. Resnick. 1987. *Economics: Marxian Versus Neoclassical.* Baltimore: Johns Hopkins University Press.

2 The family farm hybrid, feudal-ancient subsidies, and the farm woman problem

At the turn of the twentieth century, the Midwest[1] served as the nation's bread-basket, supplying cattle, hogs, wheat, corn, and dairy products. Except in Michigan and Ohio, agriculture dominated the Midwestern economy, and family-operated farms dominated the agriculture. Most farms were general farms, specializing in the crops they marketed while producing a wide variety of products for family use. Commercial crops produced on each farm were generally some combination of livestock and field crops. Corn was the major field crop in every state except North Dakota, where wheat had already gained a firm foothold. Wisconsin and Minnesota farmers were developing a specialization in dairy products, but corn and corn-fed livestock, especially corn-hog operations, were the most widespread specializations in the region.

It was at this time that the term "family farm" was first used to describe "a farm organized around the labor and economic support of a nuclear family" (Fink 1992, 28).[2] Farmers themselves, with the help of their families, did most of the work, most of the time (Fink 1992; Hurt 2003; Jellison 1993, 5; Neth 1998). The nuclear family was the primary economic, social, and educational institution in the countryside, and responsibility for the family farm's fortunes rested there. Each farm household occupied its own parcel of land, physically and socially separated from its neighbors. Even though they relied on markets to connect them to the outside world, and faced intense competitive pressures there, American farm families were more self-sufficient in comparison to both urban and European farm families (Danbom 1979). Geography and economics, among other factors, combined to both insulate and isolate family farms, providing crucial, if contradictory, conditions for their existence.

For the prominent Country Life reformer and journalist Herbert Quick, the fact that "wife and children are economic assets instead of liabilities" was a key benefit of country living (Lauters 2009). Family labor was, therefore, crucial for the viability of Midwestern agriculture. Farm men and women worked year-round from dawn to dusk, mostly without vacation, to meet the family's needs and to earn an income. Farm families could ill afford to support a family member who did not contribute, so farm children were expected to work as well. Labor was divided according to gender, with farm men largely responsible for livestock and field crops for the market, and farm women responsible for household,

Figure 2.1 Midwestern farm family, circa 1915 outside Fayette, MO (unpublished photograph from author's personal collection).

childcare, and other farm production tasks geared toward meeting the farm family's consumption needs. Farm women's income went toward the farm family's
living expenses, while men's income paid for farm equipment and supplies, livestock, and other expenses related to the commercial farm enterprise (Fink 1992).

At this point, it might be useful to provide a preliminary framework for con-
textualizing the discussion that follows in terms of class. Recall from Chapter 1
that the family farm is conceptualized as a hybrid of different kinds of class
structures, including ancient, feudal, and capitalist. Class revenues stemmed
from the surplus labor produced and appropriated in these three kinds of class
structures. Each of these revenue positions corresponded to subsumed class
expenditures to secure the necessary conditions of existence for each of the three
kinds of class structure. These class revenues and expenditures were supplemented with non-class revenues of various kinds, and non-class expenditures
required to ensure the continued receipt of these revenues. This chapter focuses
on describing the family farm's class structures, in particular that of the feudal,
along with the non-class revenues and expenditures as they arise from the
transfer of surplus between the different kinds of structures within the family
farm, especially from the feudal to the ancient.

To simplify that analysis, I disaggregate the family farm's class structure, and
consider its constituent components separately. For simplicity, I assume for now
that the family farm contained only two simple forms of class structure: the
ancient in which the labor of the farmer in the farm enterprise occurred, and the

feudal in which the labor of the farm wife in the farm enterprise and farm household occurred. I assume, for now, what was the most common case, in which the farm wife did no additional work alongside her husband with livestock or crops for commercial production in the farm enterprise biases. (Although she did perform work on her own or with her children in the farm enterprise barn and garden.) I also leave aside the labor of children and hired hands for the moment, although this will be discussed at length below. I can then map the feudal class process in which the farm wife labored in terms of feudal revenues and expenditures. Recall from Chapter 1 that a feudal class process is one in which the "lord" appropriates and distributes the surplus labor produced by his "serf." This exploitative relationship is characterized by personal ties of loyalty, obligation, and even affection. Various conditions shape the feudal relationship so that it may have existed in various times and places, and in particular historical forms, not limited to that of medieval Europe from which its name is derived. Here, I begin to excavate feudal class processes in early twentieth century Midwestern family farms.

Feudal revenues consisted of the feudal surplus labor of farm women in both the family farm household and in the family farm enterprise. This included the cooked meals, sewn clothes, and other goods and services (or the proceeds from their sale) that resulted from her household production, as well as the eggs, milk, vegetables and other goods and services (or the proceeds from their sale) that resulted from her farm production. A farm woman's labor is called "feudal" because these labor processes occurred in the context of a feudal class process, and it is "surplus" because it includes that portion of her production beyond what she needed for her own consumption in order to reproduce her feudal labor power.

Her husband, as feudal lord, was the first recipient of his wife's feudal surplus, and distributed it in order to secure the conditions of existence for the family farm's feudal class process in both the farm household and the farm enterprise. Like feudal surplus labor in the family farm's household and enterprise, these distributions, or subsumed class payments, took either a monetary or non-monetary form. Each payment represented a claim on the feudal surplus, while securing one or more conditions of existence for the continued production and appropriation of that surplus. Outlays included things like payments for property taxes, church tithes, or additional household means of production, or "volunteer" time and donated goods for local social groups and schools.[3]

Similarly, the ancient class process can be mapped in terms of its revenues and expenditures. Recall from Chapter 1 that the ancient class process is one which is self-exploitative in the sense that the producer of surplus is also its appropriator and distributor. Even though ancients may labor in physical proximity, side-by-side, they are not laboring "together" in the sense of socialized production or appropriation. That is, they are still engaged in an "independent" process characterized by individual, not communal surplus production, appropriation, and distribution. Like the feudal, various factors may condition the existence of the ancient class process at various times and places, including the turn of the twentieth century, Midwestern, family farm. Here, ancient surplus labor occurred along with the farmer's labor processes in the family farm enterprise, directed toward the production of crops and livestock for market exchange, or of the means of production for these commercial products. The farmer's labor is called "ancient" because these labor processes occurred in the context of an ancient class process, with the farmer producing and appropriating his own surplus. And it is surplus because it included the portion of the ancient farmer's production beyond what was required to reproduce his ancient labor power. Ancient surplus so produced and appropriated was available to be distributed in the form of subsumed class payments by the ancient farmer in order to secure and reproduce the conditions of existence for the ancient class process in the family farm enterprise.[4]

Additional revenues, everything being equal, could allow expanded access to conditions of existence. Likewise, a subtraction of surplus available, all else being equal, could inhibit the reproduction of the affected class structure by threatening the ability to secure one or more of its conditions of existence. Thus, expanded conditions of existence for one class structure, if these came at the expense of a subtraction of surplus available for the other, could have contradictory impacts on the family farm hybrid of these class structures, as one of its constituent class processes expanded by throwing the other into crisis. These were precisely the impacts of the transfers from the feudal to the ancient class structures in the family farm.

These transfers most commonly took two forms or strategies: "making do" and "helping out." In class analytical terms, the strategy of making do involved the many ways in which the feudal surplus labor of the farm wife was appropriated by her husband in his role as feudal lord, then transferred to his (or his workers') consumption in his role as ancient (or in his role in some form of ancient hybrid). The strategy of helping out involved the direct performance of feudal surplus labor by farm women and children in commercial farm production. The class analysis of both of these strategies and their impacts are discussed at length below.

The additional revenues thus made available were extremely important in shaping the survival and development of ancient class processes in family farms, helping ancient farmers cope with the inherent risks of farming due to weather, unstable prices, and intense competition from other farmers. Extra surplus was required to finance the conversion to the scientific methods and mechanization of ancient farm production processes promoted by the Country Life agenda and government agencies. With extra surplus, ancient farmers could purchase newly available machinery like tractors or harvesters, and/or the additional land to farm with that new equipment. If they could not purchase these items outright, extra surplus could be used to access the credit to finance expanded means of production. These increased distributions for credit, accumulation, and expansion, enabled by the increased surplus of farm women and children, were important in shaping agricultural development in the decades that followed, and will be discussed at length in the next chapter.

As mentioned in Chapter 1, the ancient class structure took priority for most family farms, shaped by ideological processes that defined the job of "farming" as such. Even though it was but one among the different kinds of class structures occurring there, the ancient class process was widely considered to be the heart of the family farm, for which its members toiled and sacrificed. Ancient farmers could not, however, generally appropriate enough surplus from their own labor to sustain and reproduce themselves as ancients. The priority placed on the ancient class process, coupled with its inability to survive on its own, created the conditions for the hybrid family farm. At the same time, that very hybrid was rendered invisible and non-ancient class structures were thereby pushed into the position of subsidizing the ancient. The discussion below will focus on how family members adjusted the feudal and ancient class structural revenues and expenditures so as to maximize the net outlays for the ancient class structure – the "real" business of the family farm, the contradictory impacts of these adjustments, and the powerful conditions of existence of the family farm hybrid, in spite of the overwhelming demands on its members.

In this chapter, I develop a model of the family farm and its interdependent class structures. I highlight the crucial role of women and children's "invisible" labor in the survival of the family farm, as well as the conflicts within family farms stemming from that role. I begin by describing the family farm's ancient class structure as it occurred along with the labor of farm men in the family farm enterprise. I describe the conditions producing the reliance of the ancient class structure on the feudal subsidies from farm women and children. I then describe the labor processes of farm women and children, and the feudal class structure in which that labor occurred. The ancient/feudal class structural hybrid was shaped by contradictory conditions of existence including important ideological processes of gender and agrarianism. The next section of the chapter discusses a selection of these processes that served to both support and undermine the family farm's class structures. I then turn to the class analytics of the value transfers between the feudal and ancient class structures comprising the family farm household and enterprise. By reconceptualizing the important practices of "making do" and "helping out" in terms of class, I show how farm women and children's labor underwrote the survival of the family farm's ancient class structures. The work of farm women and children helped insulate the ancient class processes from crisis and underwrote their expansion, because bonds of feudal obligation called forth the flexibility required to respond to, and ameliorate, crisis. Survival, even prosperity, for the family farm had its price, however, as these strategies simultaneously produced contradictory effects that threatened that very survival. The heightened contradiction that arose from the increasingly onerous and untenable burden placed on farm family members is reflected in concern for the "farm woman problem," which I revisit to conclude the chapter.

The ancient corn belt farming system and feudal-ancient subsidies

As previously mentioned, ancient farmers could not, in general, appropriate enough surplus to reproduce the necessary conditions for their continued existence as ancient farmers. Even if they could, the limitations of the ancient class process itself rendered them ill-equipped to respond to unanticipated crises or to opportunities for expansion. This issue was further exacerbated in the particular case of ancient class processes in Corn Belt farming systems during the early twentieth century. As mentioned in Chapter 1, and worth repeating here, the ancient producer is the sole source of necessary and surplus labor, hence it is not possible for his surplus to exceed his total labor. Nor is it possible for his total labor to exceed his physical limitations in performing it. Any efforts to increase either his absolute or relative surplus labor therefore come at his own expense. Increasing absolute surplus means stretching physical limits and cutting into time for rest and rejuvenation of labor power. Further, any increase in relative surplus through reduced necessary labor must come at the expense of the ancient producer's consumption, and therefore also threaten his ability to reproduce his own labor power (Gabriel 1989).

The limitations of the ancient class process in general, therefore, hobbled the ancient farmer's ability to adapt to changed circumstances. These limitations constituted a severe handicap for the ancient farmer, subject as he was to the risks of price fluctuations and intense competition in the context of relatively lengthy production processes in addition to the whims of weather, disease, insects, and animals. The inherent risks of farming participated in shaping a complex system of diversified farming in the Corn Belt at this time as one way of insuring against these and other unpredicted disasters. The increased labor requirements of such a system, however, participated in shaping the ancient farmer's dependence on the labor of others and on non-ancient class structures within the family farm, even as this system rendered him more independent vis-à-vis non-ancient class structures in the outside world because he produced a significant portion of his required means of production himself. This insulation served to increase the ancient farmer's isolation, which was further exacerbated by limited access to communication and transportation technologies. Lack of labor-saving technologies in farm and home production further contributed to long hours of work and, because of this, increased isolation from the outside world and further dependence on others inside the family farm. Finally, ideological processes that celebrated land ownership and the supposed independence accompanying it elevated the status of the land-owning ancient farmers to the uppermost rung on the socioeconomic ladder. Even though the days of free land were gone and vertical mobility was on the decline, the rags to riches mythology still persisted, bolstered by individual neighborhood examples of laborers-turned-landlords (Danbom 1979). This contributed to a shortage of available non-family labor for hire in rural areas, as those who could do so pursued this goal for themselves.

This combination of factors meant that ancient farmers simply could not purchase many of the goods and services they needed to consume, either because
they were unavailable or because they lacked easy access to markets selling
them. Furthermore, they lacked access to an abundant and reliable supply of
non-family laborers that could be hired and fired on demand. The inherent risks
of farming and the intense competition in farm commodity markets, along with
isolation and insulation, combined to produce the conditions limiting the ancient
farmer's ability to produce and appropriate enough surplus to survive on his
own. The ancient farmer required a relatively captive labor force that could be
called upon as needed to supplement his own labor in commercial farm production, as well as a means of providing for his consumption. He simply could not
do enough on his own. His continued survival as an "independent" ancient
farmer meant his dependence on non-ancient class processes within the family
farm. The addition of the feudal class process, and the formation of the ancient/
feudal hybrid that was the family farm, met those needs. Hence, this is one set of
factors shaping the existence of the family farm hybrid as a relatively stable and
long-lived, as opposed to a temporary and transitional, class structural form in
U.S. agriculture. The myth of the independent family farmer has probably
always been just that – simply a myth. As the muckraking journalists, the
Bruères, pointed out, "For, after all, a man will not live on the farm without a
wife" (Bruère and Bruère 1912).

A few details may help to illustrate the specific situation of ancient farmers in
the Corn Belt during the time period under consideration, roughly 1900 to 1940.
Farm men (and women) worked long hours each day, from dawn or before until
dusk or beyond, leaving few hours for leisure time and little room for an
extended vacation from the farm. Studies showed that farmers generally enjoyed
only about three hours of leisure time on average per working day (Vanek 1980).
Farm families rarely took vacations, and if they did, it was usually for a brief
period of time (Clark and Gray 1930). The average length of the workday for
Midwestern farmers ranged from a little less than 10 hours in the winter to
almost 13 hours in the summer, or 11 hours on average throughout the year
(Rankin 1928; Vanek 1980). Farmers (and their families) worked six days a
week, and a little less on Sundays, when they worked an average of three to six
hours (Vanek 1980). Farmers had very little time to spend in household production – cooking meals, cleaning clothes, etc. to meet their own consumption needs
– as almost all of their working time was needed for commercial farm
production.

Ancient farm enterprise systems in the Corn Belt during this time period were
complex combinations of overlapping production processes. Ancient farmers
diversified to reduce risk by producing a variety of products for sale, as well as
means of production used in the production of those products. Hence farms
usually produced a mixture of livestock and field crops for sale, as well as means
of production including fodder for livestock and draft animals. Unlike the farms
of today, which are highly specialized in either crops or livestock, and only one or
a few varieties of each, the farms of this period were general farms. Commercial

livestock included hogs and beef cattle. Commercial field crops included chiefly corn and wheat. Crops for fodder included oats, clover, alfalfa, and hay. The varieties of crops grown complemented each other in several ways. First, crops could be fed to livestock and to draft animals, which then produced manure to fertilize the crops for the next growing season. Rotating between crops and livestock, as well as among different varieties of plants, vastly improved soil fertility and reduced the need to purchase fertilizer. For example, one study of Corn Belt farms found that corn yields per acre in the Corn Belt were 36 percent higher on farms with livestock compared to those without, as the manure replenished soil fertility as livestock grazed on crop residues in fallow fields (Martini 2003). Similarly, leguminous plants like alfalfa and clover that fix atmospheric nitrogen in the soil could be grown in rotation with nitrogen-thirsty crops like corn. The complex system of crops helped reduce risk and boosted the surplus produced from the ancient farm enterprise. It also required huge amounts of labor given the horse-farming technology common at the time, particularly before the invention of the general purpose tractor in 1923.

While the variety of crops and livestock helped smooth labor requirements somewhat over the course of the year, there were still intense, brief periods during which the labor required to complete production tasks swelled beyond the ancient farmers' physical capabilities and help was necessary. Figure 2.2 and its caption, reproduced from a 1921 USDA study, show the distribution of man labor throughout the year for a typical Iowa farm, as well as the rich variety of livestock and crops grown there (Moorehouse 1921). As the figure demonstrates, livestock work was relatively steady throughout the year, aside from the seasonal requirements of birthing during the spring. The bulk of the farmer's work was concentrated in the spring, summer, late fall, and early winter during the months of plowing, planting, cultivating, and harvesting field crops and mowing hay. Corn production commanded the heaviest amounts of labor during short bursts in May for plowing and planting, and September for harvest. The labor-intensive methods used at the time during harvest illustrate why this was so. After the plowing, disking, harrowing, planting, and then cultivating three or four times throughout the summer, most farmers harvested the corn by husking it from standing stalks. The farmer, usually with the help of others, moved up and down the rows of corn picking the ears from the stalk, removing the husk, and throwing the ear into a horse-drawn wagon slowly pulled between the rows. Whereas the average labor required for all pre-harvest operations in the Corn Belt ranged between eight and thirteen hours per acre in 1919, depending on the region, harvesting from standing stalks alone required five to six hours of labor per acre. Average corn acreage was 63 (out of 135 crop acres) per farm (Macy 1938). As Figure 2.2 indicates, completing these operations required help from hired workers (if they were available) or, more commonly, from unpaid family members.

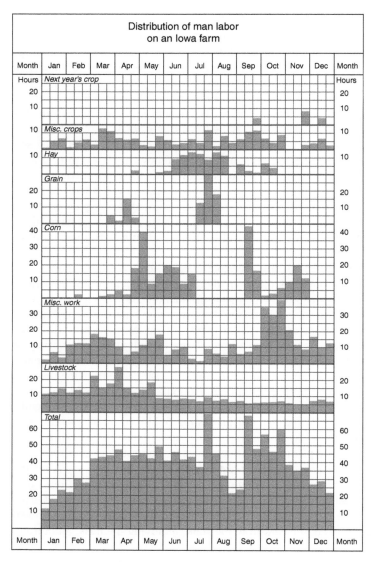

Figure 2.2 Distribution of man labor on an Iowa farm. This farm had the following crop and livestock organization: silage corn, 26.4 acres; ear corn, 69 acres; corn hogged down, 5.75 acres; oats, 26.1 acres; barley, 15.88 acres; spring wheat, 4.7 acres; winter wheat, 17 acres; clover, 13.2 acres; timothy hay, 19.3 acres; timothy seed, 17.5 acres; alfalfa, 9.3 acres; potatoes, 3.5 acres. Total crop acreage, 227.63. The following livestock was kept on the farm: horses, 14.1; cows, 6; steers, 24.2; beef cattle (breeding herd), 28.1; hogs, 16.1; making a total of 88.5 animal units. Black bars indicate average hours per day for each 10-day period (Moorhouse 1921, 55) (reprinted from Moorhouse, L.A. 1921. "Labor and Material Requirements of Field Crops". United States Department of Agriculture Bulletin No. 1000. Washington D.C.: Government Printing Office).

"Unemployed" and unpaid: what did farm wives do?

> From the experience of 30 years in the store business in rural parts of northern Minnesota, I do not hesitate to say that over one-half of the total work done on the farm has been done by the women of the house, besides they have done all their cooking and mending and have raised the families.
>
> (rural Minnesota man (USDA 1915)

The division of labor in family farms relegated the farm wife primarily to the crucial occupation of provisioning and reproducing the farm labor force, i.e. the farm family. In fact, adult women had access to farming almost exclusively through their roles as wives of farmers and mothers of future farmers and farm workers. While there were unmarried women farmers in the Midwest at the time, they were considered a neighborhood oddity, and most had inherited their farms from a husband or father (Jellison 1993). The Homestead Act of 1862 was the first to allow single women, as heads of families, to acquire their own land. Single women, nevertheless, rarely homesteaded, and, when they did, it was often in order to sell their claim for cash in order to marry (Fink 1992). Married women could not acquire their own land under the Act. According to the 1910 census, rural women were more likely to be married than any other population group in the Midwest (Jellison 1993). So enmeshed were farming and family for adult women that a "farm woman" was assumed to also be a "farm wife" (Fink 1992, 58).

Entry into marriage, then, while rendering farm women officially without occupation, was often a condition for women's entry into the "occupation" of family farming.[5] Farm women thus (un?)employed performed long hours of labor in the household, barnyard, and garden in the "important tasks of homemaking and domestic manufacturing" (USDA 1915, 5). As the Minnesota man quoted above suggested, farm women's work was significant – both in terms of the burden for the women who performed it, and in terms of its importance for sustaining the farm and family. In 1920, Florence Ward, head of the USDA's extension work with women in northern and western states, published the results of a 1919 survey of the living and working conditions of 10,000 farm women. In her introduction, she noted the "singular anomaly" that "although the census places farm women with other homemakers in a class of those having 'no occupation,' the results of the survey indicate that "the farm woman might be better described as one having ceaseless occupation, so varied and insistent are the demand made upon her" (Ward 1920, 437). She went on to list some of the roles of the average woman in the survey: "cook, seamstress, laundress, and nurse, family purchasing agent, teacher of her children, and factor in community life, as well as producer of dairy, garden, and poultry products" (Ward 1920, 438).

In addition to Ward's 1920 survey, two earlier studies were conducted by Ilena M. Bailey, a home economist with the USDA's Office of Home Economics. The first, begun in 1912, was a year-long study of farm home management in which thirteen farm women in Illinois and Indiana were asked to keep daily records. The second, with Melissa Snyder, was a 1917 investigation of ninety-one farm homes in Michigan. Ward's survey, while groundbreaking in the extent of its coverage, did not ask about time spent on specific tasks. While Bailey's work was less extensive, and even less extensively reported, it did include some of this information. Both studies included questions about the total length of the workday. Bailey's work formed the foundation for the extensive series of time-use studies of farm women (and men) funded by the 1925 Purnell Act and conducted by state agricultural experiment stations with coordination by the USDA's Bureau of Home Economics (BHE) from the late 1920s to the 1960s. The early studies were conducted under the direction of Hildegarde Kneeland, who took over the leadership of the Division of Economic Studies from Bailey and adopted her clock chart survey technique for the studies.

Taken together, the studies paint a portrait of farm women's work in Midwestern states during the early twentieth century. Like other such efforts, including the 1913 USDA survey of the wives of 55,000 volunteer crop correspondents, responses were probably skewed by survey collection methods that overrepresented the more "progressive," prosperous, native-born, and white – the elite of farm families. Time use researchers, for example, often excluded non-English speaking women from their studies (Kline 1997). In addition, completing the daily logs required significant time expenditure itself, which meant that the busier, poorer, or less literate women could not keep the records and hence were not included in the studies (Kline 1997, 370; Kneeland 1928, 620). The lives of these "elites" who were overrepresented in the studies were by no means leisurely, even by the standards of the day, as evidenced by researchers' remarks, meaning conditions were probably more difficult for the majority of women.

All studies substantiated the perception that farm women worked long hours year-round, but they were especially busy during the summer months due to their seasonal chores like gardening, canning, and helping with fieldwork. Farm women (and men) generally began the workday around 5 a.m. in the summer and 6 a.m. in the winter. They finished work around 8:30 p.m. in the summer and 7:30 p.m. in the winter with the evening chores after supper. The family was usually in bed by 10 p.m. (Bailey 1915; Bailey and Snyder 1921; Rankin 1928; Vanek 1980). In the Bailey studies, farm women were found to work between 10 and 13 hours per day, with the longer workday in the summer. The Ward study supported these findings, reporting an average length of the workday as 13.1 hours in the summer, and 10.5 in the winter (441). Other studies confirmed the average of between 10 and 11 hours per day (Vanek 1980, 424).

Farm women (and other family members) worked six days a week. Sunday was the only day of relative leisure but even then farm women worked half a day. Even though they took the day off from their usual chores like cleaning and sewing, they spent more time in meal preparation as the family often had guests and more elaborate meals on Sundays. Time use studies through the 1920s and 30s recorded an average workweek of about 62 to 64 hours for farm women (Kline 1997).[6,7] In her 1928 report on some of the time-use survey results, Kneeland noted that although "[t]here is much talk nowadays about the housewife with too much leisure" the farm woman suffered no such fate. "Of her the old saying still has significance: 'Man works from sun to sun, but woman's work is never done'" (Kneeland 1928, 620).

A farm woman's responsibilities centered around household and family maintenance, and included tasks like "dishwashing, laundry work, gathering eggs, picking fruit, and weeding the flower bed" (Bailey 1915). Regular household tasks included "preparing and serving food, keeping the house in order, caring for children, and mending," and occasional tasks included "making garments, caring for the sick, and helping out with field work in times of emergency" (Bailey and Snyder 1921, 353). The Ward survey assumed that all farm women did housecleaning, and asked only for how many rooms they cared. (The average was 7.8). Over 90 percent of women did their own laundry (96 percent), sewing (92 percent), and bread baking (94 percent).

Table 2.1 lists time spent on "home-making" tasks for the representative farm woman from a 1928 BHE study. Food preparation tasks consumed the most time, followed by clothing and care of the house. Home-making tasks also included child care and "purchasing, planning, and management." Overall, household production consumed about 53 hours per week for the average farm woman in the study (Kneeland 1928).

These labor-intensive tasks were made more so for the majority of women whose homes lacked electric lighting or power and who therefore carried coal or wood for heating and cooking, and water for washing and bathing. Most farm homes lacked such labor-saving "modern improvements" as "running water, hot

Table 2.1 Distribution of hours per week for "home-making"

Task	Hours
Preparing meals	16.2
Clearing meals	8.5
Food preservation	0.9
Other food work	0.2
Food total	**25.9**
Cleaning and straightening house	8.3
Care of house	2.3
House total	**10.5**
Laundry	5.4
Sewing	4.2
Mending	1.8
Other clothing care	**0.2**
Clothing total	**11.5**
Care of children and others	**2.4**
Purchasing, planning, and management	**1.8**
Misc.	**0.9**
TOTAL	**53.0**

Source: Data from Kneeland, Hildegarde. 1928. "Women on Farms Average 63 Hours' Work Weekly in Survey of 700 Homes." In *Yearbook of Agriculture 1928*, 620–622. Washington, D.C.: Government Printing Office.

water, a set bathtub, some system of sewerage, gas or electric lights, and furnace," even though these were common in urban homes by this time. Table 2.2 below presents data on these items from the Michigan and Ward studies. Only two of the 91 homes in the 1917 Michigan study had all of these conveniences. Most farms used kerosene lighting, coal or wood stoves for cooking, and coal, wood, or oil burning stoves for heat. Only 60 percent of the houses had kitchen sinks – but not necessarily sinks with drains and sewerage systems. 78 percent emptied waste water in the back yard. The Ward survey confirmed that most farm women performed their duties without the help of this type of modern equipment. Seventy-nine percent used kerosene lanterns, 32 percent had running water, only 60 percent had a sink with a drain, and 61 percent were responsible for carrying the water they used. Ninety percent of farm homes had outdoor toilets. Only 22 percent had power machinery of any kind, including the 57 percent who had washing machines. Kerosene lanterns and wood stoves increased the work of cleaning, as did the grassless, dirt backyards gracing most farm homes, but one of the most onerous chores was the laundry, a strenuous task that in typical farm homes was reserved for one single and entire day (Neth 1998, 27). Laundry meant heating, carrying, filling, and emptying buckets of water; scrubbing, rinsing, and wringing fabrics, or turning a heavy hand-cranked device. The Michigan women spent an average of 7.25 hours per week on laundry. As Nellie Kedzie Jones noted in a 1914 *Country Gentleman* column, "I wish it could be burnt into the consciousness of every man and every woman that washing under average farm conditions is man's work, not a woman's"

Table 2.2 Equipment in farm homes surveyed, 1917 and 1919

	Bailey and Snyder, Michigan 1917, 91 homes	Ward, 33 Northern and Western States 1919, 10,044 homes
Lighting	88% kerosene lamps, 11% gas, 1% electric	79% kerosene lamps, 21% unspecified
Heating	82% stoves, 18% furnaces	Not Reported
Cooking	88% wood; 12% wood and coal and 74% also oil or gas	Not Reported
Water	24% with running water	32% with running water
Kitchen sinks	55% with water in the house; 60% with kitchen sinks	65% water in kitchen; 60% sink and drain
Outdoor toilet	90% with outdoor toilet	90% with outdoor toilet
Fixed bathtub	19% (14% with hot water boilers)	20%
Sewer system	22% with septic tank or cess pool; 78% emptied water in the back yard	Not Reported

Sources: Data from Bailey, Ilena M., and Snyder, Melissa F. 1921. "A Survey of Farm Homes." *The Journal of Home Economics* 13 (8): 346–356 and Ward, Florence. 1920. "The Farm Woman's Problems." *The Journal of Home Economics* 12 (10) (October): 437–457.

(Kleinegger 1988, 171). By the 1928 BHE study 10 years later, in spite of efforts to promote labor-saving technologies for farm homes, farm women had managed to knock less than two hours per week from the time devoted to laundry (5.4 hours).

Farm women's customary responsibilities, unlike those of urban women, often extended to the barn, henhouse, dairy, orchard and garden to include work in the farm enterprise. Such work commonly included caring for animals, especially poultry and dairy cows, as well as vegetable gardens and orchards. The women in Figure 2.3 are gathering wild berries. These activities produced eggs, milk, cream, cheese and butter, fresh, dried, and canned fruits and vegetables, jams and jellies.

The Michigan women spent an average of two hours a day on the "special kinds of work" associated with dairying (including making butter), gardening,

Figure 2.3 Farm women gathering berries, circa 1915 outside Fayette, MO (unpublished photograph from author's personal collection).

and poultry work. All farms surveyed kept cows, poultry, and gardens. Most (75 percent) reported orchards as well. In Ward's survey, 67 percent of women in the Central states cared for gardens, 89 percent cared for poultry, 45 percent helped milk cows, and 93 percent washed milk pails. A majority of women, 66 percent, made their own butter.[8] Figure 2.4 documents what Kneeland (1928, 620) referred to as the farm woman's "double job" – "farmer as well as home maker." Like other studies, this one from 1932 showed that farm and urban homemakers spent roughly equal amounts of time in home production activities, or "home making," yet urban women enjoyed approximately nine extra hours for leisure, sleep, and rest than farm women, due to the addition of "farm work" among the customary tasks of the latter (Kneeland 1932).

In addition to providing products and services directly for family consumption, thereby providing for a large share of the family's subsistence needs, women often sold their products for cash. This income was directed toward meeting the needs of the farm family. Ninety percent of the farm women in the Michigan study reported income from the sale of poultry, eggs, and dairy products. The Michigan women considered the income from their activities as "belonging distinctly to the home" (Bailey and Snyder 1921, 355). According to Neth (1998), "the connection between women's income and its use for family purchases appears almost universal." Egg, chicken, and butter money were often said to have "bought the groceries" which included cereal products, coffee, tea, meat, and sugar. Other commonly purchased items included fabric, some

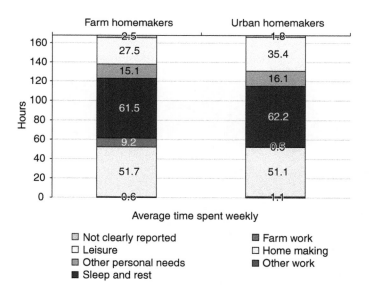

Figure 2.4 Average weekly distribution of time: farm and urban homemakers, 1932 (data from Kneeland, Hildegarde. 1932. "Leisure of Home Makers Studied for Light on Standards of Living." In *Yearbook of Agriculture 1932*, 562–564. Washington, D.C.: Government Printing Office).

clothing, shoes, heating and cooking fuel, medicine, and medical services. Women in the Ward survey similarly reported marketing poultry and dairy products while not keeping the earnings for their own use. For example, only 9 percent of the 33 percent of women in the Central states who made butter to sell had the butter money for their own use. Similarly, while 89 percent of farm women cared for poultry, only 25 percent had poultry money, and 16 percent had egg money for their own use.

Women's household production played a significant role in maintaining the living standards of farm families. Bailey's Michigan study showed that 80 percent of the living expenditures for the farm family "were met by the extra household activities of the housekeepers, leaving only 20 percent to be contributed from the proceeds of the principal products of the farm" (Bailey and Snyder 1921, 356). They noted that this, plus her unpaid labor time, showed that the farm wife made a significant contribution to the "economic support of the family as well as to its comfort and well-being" (Bailey and Snyder 1921). A study of 2,886 farm families in 11 states from 1922 to 1924 found that the farms furnished an average of 43 percent of the total value of goods for household use, including 67 percent of the total value of food consumed (Kirkpatrick 1929, 56–57). A study of 147 Iowa families between 1926 and 1929 found that these families supplied three-fifths of their own food, including 95 percent of poultry, milk, eggs, and cream, 81 percent of meat, and 43 percent of vegetables (Neth 1998).

In addition to their work in household, barn, henhouse, and garden production, meeting the family's subsistence needs and reproducing the farm labor force, Midwestern farm wives sometimes engaged in the production of cash crops – non-dairy livestock, field crops and related activities – working alongside their husbands and other workers. In the Ward survey, 25 percent of women helped with non-dairy livestock and 24 percent helped in the field for an average of seven weeks in the year. According to Neth, the biases of the study mean these and other figures related to women's outdoor work are probably low estimates, since the more "progressive" farms (probably overrepresented in the survey) were more likely to maintain a more strict gender division of labor (Neth 1998, 19–20). In addition, the construction of surveys was conditioned by the constructions of gender and ideas regarding the appropriate spheres of male and female work. Bailey's 1912 study, for example, did not enumerate tasks such as field work or helping with livestock among the labor classifications farm women could choose from (Kline 1997; Bailey 1915). According to a 1927–1928 study of Nebraska farm women, 35 percent reported doing some kind of outside farm work other than caring for chickens, gardens, and milking. These tasks included haying, corn husking, plowing, driving the hay rake, shocking grain, cultivating corn, harrowing, repairing fences, and running the tractor (Clark and Gray 1930, 25). Some farm women undertook these tasks as part of their regular work. For others, this work was more contingent and irregular, undertaken as "an unusual task which arose because of the illness or absence of the husband, son, or hired man, or because of an unusual amount of farm work at certain seasons of the year" (Clark and Gray 1930, 25). Some women reported enjoying this type of work, and others said they preferred doing it rather than boarding and lodging a hired hand in the house. Women's work in this type of farm production was often described as "helping out." Table 2.3 summarizes the above discussion of farm women's work as described by the 1919 Ward survey.

Family farm feudalism

How, then, are we to interpret farm women's work in terms of class? Consider the following letter by Mrs. E.G.R. of Michigan to *The Farmer's Wife* in 1924 exclaiming at the "blessing" of having "an allowance." She reasoned that her regular work, "if paid for at a conservative price, would amount to more in a month than I had been spending on my personal self in a year." She concluded, "You would smile at the amount of this wonderful allowance but it is all mine and just because I haven't had anything except in common with the family, it seems munificent to me" (E.G.R. 1924, 181). Her efforts at persuading herself, her husband, and the readers of the magazine that she deserved some money of her own seem to confirm the absence of self or communal appropriation of her surplus. As her letter indicates, she was not expecting, nor had she been, regularly compensated for her work, which involved providing for herself and for her family.

A farm wife's work was unpaid, and the use values she produced took the form of services like childcare and cleaning, products like cooked meals and sewn shirts, and cash from the sale of products like butter and eggs. One farm woman from Kansas wrote in response to the 1913 USDA survey of the wives of crop correspondents and asked, "When I have cooked, and swept, and washed, and ironed, and made beds for a family of five (two small children), and have done the necessary mending and some sewing, haven't I done enough?" (USDA 1915, 51). As this statement indicates, farm women produced use values not only for themselves, but also for other family members including their husbands and children. Their responsibilities in the farm household and farm enterprise were delineated largely according to their gender, and largely completed without expecting or receiving assistance from their husbands. A farm woman performed necessary labor, the fruits of which she received back to reproduce her labor power. In addition, she worked to produce more than what was socially necessary for her own reproduction. In doing so, she performed surplus labor, the fruits of which were appropriated and distributed by someone other than herself. Her husband, described as "lord and master" of the family farm was that person (*The Ladies' Home Journal* 1909). As one woman from Nebraska wrote, "One of the most necessary aids to the farmer's wife is that she should have the fruits of her labor. Hers is a life of toil just as long as she remains on the farm" (*The Ladies' Home Journal* 1909, 50). One farm woman from Oregon specifically noted the difference between her situation and that of her husband or even his hired workers:

Table 2.3 Farm women's duties, 1919

Household	Percent of women	Barnyard and garden	Percent of women	Other farm and field	Percent of women
Kerosene lamps	79	Help milk	36	Help with livestock	25
Water to carry	61	Wash pails	88	Help in Field	24
Washing/ironing	96	Make butter	60		
Sewing	92	Sell butter	33		
Bread baking	94	Caring for poultry	81		
		Caring for gardens	56		

Source: Data from Ward, Florence. 1920. "The Farm Woman's Problems." *The Journal of Home Economics* 12 (10) (October): 437–457.

The farmer may aid a great deal by sticking to the 10-hour labor system, which will lighten the labor of the woman on the farm. [T]he husband doesn't mind the long hours of labor because he thinks when he harvests the crop he will get his pay. The hired man gets paid for his work, but the tired housewife on the farm merely gets her board and clothing, the same as the farmer's work animals.

(*The Ladies' Home Journal* 1909, 52)

Much of farm women's labor, then, occurred along with an exploitative fundamental class process. Not only was farm women's work productive of surplus, but this surplus was appropriated by someone other than its direct producer. Building on the model of household feudalism developed and extended by Fraad, Resnick and Wolff (Fraad et al. 1994; Resnick and Wolff 2009), I identify this type of gendered class process as a feudal class process in which the farm wife personified the role of serf, and her husband that of lord. This form of exploitative class process is neither capitalist nor slave. While farm women may have delivered surplus or received necessary labor in monetary form, wage labor relationships were notably absent from relationships among farm husbands and wives. Neither are the direct producers the property of the appropriators, hence the feudal designator for the class process. Farm wives did not opt to go on strike or walk out in the same way that capitalist workers might have when faced with similar working conditions. In fact, they may have felt their feudal exploitation was a necessary demonstration of their familial love and service for which the return of that love and appreciation was ample compensation (Ward 1920). The connection between farm wives and husbands as producers and appropriators of surplus labor in family farms was supported by various economic, political, cultural, and natural conditions and obligations. As feudal serfs, farm women were tied to their exploiters by "marital oaths, ideology, tradition, religion, and power" (Fraad et al. 1994, 7). In addition, such conditions included important cultural processes producing gender and agrarian identities. A selection of these processes will be discussed further below. First, I discuss the role of children as serfs on the family farm.

Children as serfs

As discussed above, the typical family farm included a feudal class structure, with farm wives working in its farm household and environs, such as the barnyard, garden, orchards, henhouse, and dairy. Not only the farmer's wife, but also his children constituted a reserve labor force that could be called upon as needed. Children's labor was also typically part of the feudal class processes as children were usually integrated as additional serfs in both household and farm production. While the simple fact of work was perhaps the most striking attribute of Midwestern farm children's serfdom in general in the early twentieth century, this shared attribute was mediated by a child's individual circumstances, including gender, age, birth order, and ethnicity, as well as the economic position of their families.

Child labor on family farms was ubiquitous during the early twentieth century. Even though all 48 states had child labor restrictions and compulsory education laws in place by 1920, there were numerous exceptions and loopholes for family farms.[9] Millions of farm children were employed in agriculture and most on their own parents' farms. The 1920 census found that even in midwinter, when farm work requirements were at their lowest, nearly 650,000 children between the ages of 10 and 15 were working on the nation's 6.5 million farms. Of these, 88 percent were assisting their parents on home farms (McGill and Merritt 1929). In addition to contributing their labor services directly through labor on home farms, older farm children also commonly contributed indirectly through labor exchanges with neighbors, or by sending cash home from off-farm employment, usually on nearby farms.[10]

The prevalence and importance of child labor on family farms, as well as the gender and age differentiation of work assignments, was demonstrated by J. O. Rankin's 1928 study of Nebraska farm homes. He found that two-thirds of the 368 children over three years of age performed some type of daily work. The proportion of children working ranged from only 24 percent of those aged four to six, to 95 percent of those over 14. A slightly larger proportion of girls than boys did daily work (70 percent of girls compared to 63 percent of boys), and girls began work at a younger age. While only 18 percent of boys four to six years old did work, almost one-third of girls in that age range did work (Rankin 1928).

As indicated, chores were assigned to children as young as three or four. A 1919 article in *The Farmer's Wife* warned against the dangers of "mischievous idle hands," and advised readers that "even the three-year-old would be better and happier if he had his wee errands to run" (Tuttle 1919). Tasks were not differentiated by gender as they were for older children, and both boys and girls helped their mothers, who taught and oversaw their work, with simple chores in the household, barn, and garden. Such tasks included wiping dishes, carrying kindling, feeding chickens, gathering eggs, picking berries, planting seeds, and weeding the garden. One mother of two young children wrote to *The Farmer's Wife*, explaining that her three-year-old boy "brings in most of the wood in his wagon." Furthermore, she boasted, "on wash day I set the basket of clothes on his wagon and he follows me as I hang things on the line. It saves me bending over every time and he is so proud" (L.R.H. 1914). The cover of the magazine from that same issue, reproduced in Figure 2.5 below, depicted a cozy scene of a toddler boy helping his mother plant a garden while the dog looked on, a shade tree and large house in the background. Young children may also have been assigned to care for small, sick, or orphaned animals that might otherwise have died, or even to herd larger animals in order to save on expenses for fencing (Riney-Kehrberg 2005) The variety of work a young child could perform is indicated in an October 1926 article in *The Farmer's Wife* entitled "The Child's Work" which advised that "the country child ought to be given tools." Boy or girl, the youngster's tool kit should include "spades, rakes, hoes, a light wheelbarrow, a stout wagon, a watering can, a trowel," as well as "a couple of good

Figure 2.5 Toddler "helping out" (reprinted from *The Farmer's Wife*, April 1914. Front cover. Image provided by the Minnesota Historical Society).

hammers, a saw, a plane, a screw driver, a good knife and a fine pair of scissors" (Patri 1926).

Older girls and boys took on gendered assignments as serf-apprentice wives and farmers to their mothers and fathers, respectively. Older boys took on work in the farm fields, with livestock and operating farm machinery, and girls remained to specialize in the tasks their mothers performed as farm wife serf-apprentices in the household, barnyard, and garden. In Rankin's 1928 study of Nebraska farm homes, 94 percent of boys over the age of fourteen did outdoor work, including care of animals, gardening, and other chores, while 85 percent of older girls did housework, mostly ironing, cleaning, helping with meals, and other kinds of housework. Only about one-third of girls helped with the care of younger children. A USDA study of 559 homemakers published in 1930 verified that farm women received most (4.5 of the average of 9.25 hours per week) of the childcare help they received from their daughters (and other female relatives). The rest was from farm husbands (2 hours), sons (1.25 hours), hired help (1 hour), and guests (0.5 hours). Caring for the children was found to be almost exclusively the wife's domain, with very little help from family members, even daughters (Moore, R. 1930).

While girls' main responsibilities usually revolved around "helping ma," they could be called upon when necessary to "help pa." If no suitable older male children were available, an older girl might be assigned the role of "father's boy" (Neth 1998, 24–25). In addition to birth order and age distribution of children, ethnicity could impact children's work assignments as well. Women and girls of German, Polish and Scandinavian descent more often worked in the fields than those of English ancestry (Sherbon and Moore 1919). Just as with grown farm women, fieldwork was generally considered to be inappropriate for girls. The work of popular writers such as Hamlin Garland reflected this sentiment. In his short stories, only the "deprived daughters of the foreign born worked in the fields" while the daughters of the native born adhered to "proper" gender roles (Riney-Kehrberg 2005, 39). Necessity often trumped the distaste for girls working in the fields, especially during the busy times of planting and harvest. As a result, many farm families turned to younger sons and daughters to help in the field alongside older sons if needed, regardless of their ethnicity.

While work assignments were somewhat flexible for girls, the same was not true for boys, indicating both the subordinate status of the farm household and of "women's work." Rankin found that girls of all ages were three times more likely to do farm work than boys were to do housework. While 59 percent of girls over 14 helped with farm work, only 3 percent of boys of the same age helped in the house (1928). The indoor work of boys was often the result of the lack of suitable daughters to perform these tasks, or of the nature of the particular tasks. Washing heavy items like quilts, beating carpets, or operating the lever on a manual washing machine may have required extra strength to complete (Riney-Kehrberg 2005).

Teenagers, if not performing their usual unpaid labor on the family farm, were expected to work on neighboring farms, either for hire or as part of a labor exchange, contributing any wages toward their own necessities and to the farm enterprise (Williams and Skinner 1926; Neth 1993, 20–21). This, too, varied by gender. Almost one-fifth of older boys in the Nebraska study worked away from home on neighboring farms. Only 4 percent of older girls did so (Rankin 1928). A Children's Bureau study of child labor on farms in three Illinois counties conducted in 1923, and broadly representative of the variety of Corn Belt farms across the Midwest, found that while most children worked only for their own parents, about 40 percent also assisted neighboring farmers, and only 3 percent worked exclusively as hired laborers. Of these 25 children, only four were girls (Williams and Skinner 1926).

The authors of the Children's Bureau study noted farmers' increasing reliance on their children's labor due to economic necessity. The growing scarcity of hired labor caused by migration from rural areas, as well as the "lack of ready cash resulting from recent hard times" meant that most farm families had to make do with the unpaid hands they had available (Williams and Skinner 1926, 33). The study of "the work of children on Illinois farms," focused exclusively on the work of helping the ancient farmer/father in the production of commercial crops in the family farm enterprise. In the case of Corn Belt family farms, this type of work was referred to as "field work." (The report's authors apparently assumed that "work on farms" was synonymous with this type of work, and did not consider the work of children in helping out the farm wife/mother in feudal household or farm production.) Most of the children in the study were farmers' children of native white parentage.

Figure 2.6 shows the age and gender distribution of farm children doing field-work for the three Illinois counties included in the study. Of the 1,672 children

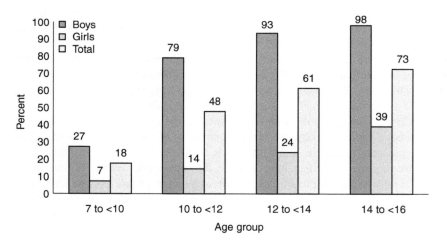

Figure 2.6 Percentage of children doing field work by age and gender (data from Williams, Dorothy, and Mary E. Skinner. 1926. "Work of Children on Illinois Farms". Department of Labor, Children's Bureau 168. Washington, D.C.: Government Printing Office).

interviewed, 737 (44 percent) of them had done field work during the year preceding the interviews, which were conducted during the spring and summer of
1923. While only about one-quarter (27 percent) of boys under 10 had done field
work, the percentage of boys doing fieldwork increased sharply for older boys so
that 79 percent of boys between 10 and 12, and nearly all (98 percent) of the
boys 12 and over had done field work. The percentage of girls doing field work
in each age group was much lower than for boys, but still significant, particularly
for girls 12 and older. Nearly one-quarter (24 percent) of girls between 12 and
14, and 39 percent of girls between 14 and 16 had done field work.

Field work began early in the spring with plowing and field preparation, and
continued intermittently throughout the summer until the harvest was completed
in late fall or early winter. While the duration of work was therefore limited,
with most children working from one to two months, their hours each day were
generally long. Table 2.4 below shows the number of hours of field work on a
typical day by age group and total. Few children (8.9 percent) worked less than
eight hours, and the most common working day for all but children under 12 was
10 hours or more. Even younger children worked a full day; over half (61.2
percent) worked eight hours or more. About two-fifths (39.1 percent) of the children between 12 and 14, and half (50.2 percent) of the children between 14 and
16 worked 10 hours or more. Children kept up long hours of work even during
harvest season when school was in session and daylight hours were shorter. For
example, children commonly participated in husking corn, which was completed
at the end of the harvest in late fall or early winter. Only 13 percent of the children who reported husking corn on a typical day reported a working day of less
than six hours. As the report's authors explained, these children typically husked
corn for a few hours before and after school, as well as all day on Saturdays.
Time spent doing chores instead of field work was not included in the "working
day," even though most children in the study reported having to do chores
as well.

Children reported doing a variety of tasks related to general farm work, the
corn crop, the hay crop, and grains other than corn. Table 2.5 below lists the
specific tasks which significant numbers of children did. Plowing and disking

Table 2.4 Number of hours of field work of children on a typical day, percentage of each
age group and totals; Illinois grain-growing region

	Total (%)	Under 12 (%)	12-under 14 (%)	14-under 16 (%)	Not reported (%)
Under 8 hours	8.9	12.2	7.4	5.9	20.0
8 to under 10 hours	34.9	33.2	36.1	35.6	40.0
10 to over 12 hours	38.0	28.0	39.1	50.2	20.0
Hours not reported	18.3	26.6	17.4	8.3	20.0

Adapted from McGill, Nettie Pauline, and Ella Arvilla Merritt. 1929. "Children in Agriculture".
Department of Labor, Children's Bureau 114. Washington, D.C.: Government Printing Office. Available online at http://archive.org/details/childreninagricu00mcgi.

Table 2.5 Farm operations performed by children of specified ages and totals

Kind of work	Total		Age (Number)			
	Percent	Number	7-under 12	12-under 14	14-under 16	Not reported
Total	100.0	737	278	243	211	5
Plowing	47.5	350	85	126	137	2
Harrowing	66.9	493	158	173	159	3
Disking	45.9	338	85	122	130	1
Hoeing	26.7	197	75	61	58	3
Cultivating corn	66.8	492	148	170	171	3
Husking corn	65.9	486	172	163	149	2
Raking hay	43.4	320	71	115	132	2
Shocking grain	43.6	321	97	110	113	1
Hauling water	42.3	312	140	124	47	1

Adapted from Williams, Dorothy, and Mary E. Skinner. 1926. "Work of Children on Illinois Farms." Department of Labor, Children's Bureau 168. Washington, DC: Government Printing Office.

Note
Totals do not add to 100 because some children did more than one kind of field work.

were among the hardest and most dangerous kinds of work that farm children did. Lightweight children could easily be thrown from the seat of the horse-drawn machines as they moved over the rough ground and, in the case of disking, impaled under the moving disks. As a consequence, it was mostly older boys who helped out with these tasks. Almost half of all children reported doing plowing and disking, and of these children, nearly three-quarters were boys between twelve and sixteen. Harrowing (or smoothing the surface of the soil after plowing or disking) was less dangerous, though still tiring. This and hoeing were more often done by younger children and older girls as well as older boys. Almost every child in the study who did field work reported helping out with the corn crop (709 of the 737 children). Children's work on the corn crop consisted mostly of cultivating and husking. Most children helped with cultivating and husking (66.8 and 65.9 percent of children, respectively). Cultivating was time-consuming, as the corn crop usually required three or four cultivations to control weeds during the growing season. Husking corn, as previously discussed, was done at harvest time when corn was picked from standing stalks. Children helped with the husking afterwards, and while the work was not difficult, it had to be done after the first heavy frost, which "often adds great discomfort to the job" (Williams and Skinner 1926, 43). In addition, inexperienced huskers could easily injure a wrist. Children also helped with the hay crop. A significant proportion (43.4 percent) raked hay, which was simple work requiring driving a team and operating simple levers. Raking hay was reported by a fifth of the girls and half of the boys, including young children. Other significant tasks that children per-formed involved the production of grains other than corn. Many children (43.6 percent) participated in shocking grains, or gathering the bundles of cut grain into piles and standing them on end in the field. Finally, significant numbers of children, particularly younger ones, participated in hauling water during thresh-ing, either to workers for drinking, or to threshing machines for the steam engine (Williams and Skinner 1926).

As the discussion above indicates, Midwestern farm children labored long hours alongside their fathers, mothers, brothers, and sisters, sometimes under harsh and dangerous conditions, at tasks that were often strenuous, tedious, or both. The conditions of farm children's lives are all the more striking because they contrasted with the experience of growing numbers of urban children, as well as increasingly dominant ideologies of childhood and family. These con-ceptions had evolved throughout the nineteenth century along with the rise of an urban middle class in which male breadwinners could earn enough to support the entire family comfortably. Even though not all, or even most, urban families shared this circumstance, the middle class experience was the dominant ideal influencing all families' aspirations as well as state policies. By 1920, the "right to childhood" was widely recognized. In this conception, childhood was a time of education and play. School and home were a child's place, not the workplace or factory floor.

The experience of most farm families, however, was still one in which the labor of all family members was expected and required. The farm family remained a primary production unit, household and enterprise intertwined, with a corresponding understanding of the role of children. As discussed above, most farm families could not afford to rely on hired labor, nor could they afford to support family members who did not "earn their keep." As rural sociologist Josiah Galpin explained, one of the primary social roles of the rural child was as an economic asset to the farm family (Galpin 1918). While increasing numbers of urban families could afford the luxury of "emotionally priceless" but "economically useless" children, rural families could not (Riney-Kehrberg 2005).

Rural children's serfdom, then, was conditioned by membership in the farm family. Like their mothers, farm children labored in the context of a feudal class process, performing both necessary and surplus labor, and delivering the fruits of that labor to one or both of their parents. Their labor was largely unpaid, as chores, housework, and fieldwork were "part of the child's share of family responsibilities and duties" (Williams and Skinner 1926, 37–38). As discussed above, even when children worked on neighboring farms they were often unpaid, and worked as part of an exchange of labor services. Those children who did work for hire were expected to contribute their wages to the family as a whole. Legally, a child's "wages and efforts" belonged to his or her parents until marriage or the age of twenty-one (Riney-Kehrberg 2005). Children could not leave to seek "employment" elsewhere unless such action was sanctioned by their parents. As mentioned above, agricultural workers were exempt from child labor legislation, and compulsory education laws had numerous loopholes "for cause" or were poorly enforced (McGill and Merritt 1929). Parental expectations and authority, along with rural isolation, therefore combined to support rural children's serfdom. Rural children were left almost completely in their parents' hands.

The farm husband/father typically retained the subsumed class decision-making role of assigning older children to help with the production of farm commodities like field crops and livestock. Since these requirements usually superseded those of the farm household, this meant he also retained authority over household production indirectly, if not directly. Alternatively, the farm wife may have served as the feudal appropriator of her children's surplus, while at the same time lacking some or all subsumed class managerial authority over these arrangements. Similarly, the farm husband may have served as the feudal appropriator of surplus, while his wife claimed managerial authority over these arrangements in household, barn, and garden production.

Evidence suggests that farm women managed the surplus of their young children when they could. In her study of Nebraska farm women from 1880 to 1940, Deborah Fink places the farm woman in the role of "buffer between her husband's desire for child labor and her children's needs (Fink 1992, 151). She also describes how farm women assigned "women's work" to their daughters and younger sons. Census takers found that farm men often did not know the basic demographic information about the members of their household, indicating that this "accounting" was part of a farm wife's responsibilities.

However, farm women probably experienced conflicted feelings about serving as feudal appropriator of their children's labor themselves, even if familial arrangements allowed this, as a means of easing the demands of their own feudal serfdom. Young children required an incredible amount of labor, especially in households that lacked running water and electricity, yet children also offered respite from the isolation, loneliness, and dependency of farm women's feudal serfdom. Given the burden of farm women's work, however, could they help but exploit them to ease their own labor once their children were old enough? Children were impacted by their mother's work requirements, even from before birth, and vice versa. Studies of maternal health in the Midwest indicated that standard practice for Midwestern farm women was to continue to work throughout pregnancy, right up to the day of confinement, and to resume work within 10 days, often less. One woman in Wisconsin was found by surveyors the day after her delivery attempting to make biscuits in bed (Moore, E. 1917; Sherbon and Moore 1919). Motherly love, and the desire to preserve a "right to childhood" may have placed limits on children's exploitation, but accounts of working conditions of orphans, even if they were extended family members, suggests that motherly and fatherly love was limited (Riney-Kehrberg 2005). Physical and economic exigencies for most farm families meant that many children probably endured dual serfdom – to their mothers and to their fathers who appropriated the surplus they produced. I now turn to discussing a selection of the ideological and other conditions of the family farm hybrid, including farm women's and children's serfdom there.

Conditions of existence for the family farm hybrid

As the discussion above makes clear, farm life was hard for everyone involved in it. Farm men, women, and children worked long hours doing strenuous work, for minimal and uncertain compensation. The ancient/feudal hybrid class structure was a stable form, yet the very strategies undertaken for its survival threw it constantly into a potential state of crisis. Powerful countervailing forces must have been at work to prevent the family farm from collapsing altogether under the weight of its inhabitants' exhaustion and the demands of their class positions. In this section, I discuss a selection of these forces, or conditions of existence for the family farm hybrid and its constituent ancient and feudal class structures. Cultural, economic, political, and natural processes combined to provide conditions of existence for farm wives and their children to occupy the class positions of serfs and their husbands that of lords as well as ancient farmers. These processes participated in producing feudal dependence for farm women and children, and the ancient independence of their farmer husbands/fathers. Because the family farm hybrid existed in constant contradiction and potential crisis, its conditions of existence both supported and undermined it at the same time.

Farm families in need of some sort of compensation for their hardships found that compensation in ideological processes which defined their identity as farm families. Like the followers of Protestantism, farmers and their families were promised a reward for their hard work and hard life. Unlike Protestants, however, farm families did not have to wait until death to enjoy their exalted status; they were living the dream – the American dream that is – on earth. As historian David Danbom explains, "To justify their choice to themselves and to others, and to mask the hard realities of farm life, rural people often embraced a series of sentimental half-truths, symbols, and myths about themselves" (Danbom 1979, 20). The organizing principle for this mythology was that of agrarianism.

Agrarianism is "the belief in the moral and economic primacy of farming over other industry, and the celebration of farming and farmers as the heart of American society" (Fink 1992, 11). Agrarianism affirmed the superiority of farmers over non-farmers as individuals, and of agriculture over industry, in the social order. Thus, agrarianism shaped the way farm men and women understood their lives and their role in society, and therefore how and whether they recognized their roles in exploitative class processes.

The notion of the essential virtue possessed by farmers, and cultivated through the practice of farming as a way of life, has been woven into the fabric of collective American identity since Jeffersonian times. It was the independent, yeoman farmer working the land he owned who served as the foundation for Thomas Jefferson's vision of democracy – both economic and political – in America. For Jefferson, the independent small producer possessed all of the virtues necessary to serve as the founding citizen of a great nation. "Those who labour in the earth," he wrote "are the chosen people of God ... whose breasts he has made his peculiar deposit for substantial and genuine virtue" (Jefferson 1853).

Agrarian mythology affirmed the economic, political, and cultural superiority of farming. A common economic view of farmers was that they performed the most basic, legitimate occupation, forming the basis of prosperity for industry, and that all other pursuits were somehow parasitic. This is closely related to the Physiocratic view that all true wealth comes from the land. William Jennings Bryan expressed this sentiment in his famous Cross of Gold Speech at the 1896 Democratic convention in Chicago when he warned, "Burn down your cities and leave our farms, and your cities will spring up again as if by magic; but destroy our farms and the grass will grow in the streets of every city in the country." Politically, farmers enjoyed the status of serving as the foundation for the republic and, in the urbanizing and industrializing nation, as the stabilizing middle class between capital and labor. As one Ohio spokesman explained, "The prosperity, peace and greatness of our American republic rests with the ... American farmer" (Danbom 1979, 21). Finally, farmers were viewed as the guardians and representatives of American virtue. "The country home is the safe anchored foundation of the Republic. It is the fountain-head of purity and strength, and will nourish and sustain the virtue and wisdom of this nation forever," proclaimed one agricultural booster (Danbom 1979, 22). Family farmers were therefore not mere "ordinary" citizens, but the very embodiment of "American-ness" for everyone, not just for themselves. Farming was not an occupation, but a way of life. Preserving the family farm meant not only providing for the farm family, but also preserving and nurturing a national resource to be passed down through the generations to come.

The mythology of agrarianism helped mask the realities of rural living and the hard work of family farming, and wrapped farmers and their families in self-congratulatory images of their lives so that they could view their work as legitimate and rewarding instead of horrifying. This provided an important support for both the ancient and feudal class processes. For the ancient farmer/feudal lord, it defined him culturally, politically, and economically as an independent producer, citizen, and head of family. For the feudal farm wife, it meant she was less likely to recognize or rebel against her exploited class position in the farm household, viewing it instead with a sense of service and fulfillment. For farm children, who often worked long hours at the expense of their formal education, it meant their labor was viewed as virtuous and educational, an affirmation of industry, thrift, and independence, rather than an abusive and exploitative violation of childhood.[11] The agrarian ideal also shaped the primacy of the ancient producer as the "real" farmer and the heart of the family farm.

Agrarianism shaped and was shaped by other significant ideological currents of the early twentieth century, including notions of gender, domesticity, and motherhood, as well as scientific racism and nationalism. Together, these ideological currents found expression through a variety of reform efforts, such as the Country Life and eugenics movements, and informed the mission of government agencies such as the USDA Extension Service, the Bureau of Home Economics, and the Children's Bureau. By the turn of the twentieth century, the American family was widely seen to be in crisis. By the late 1800s, the U.S. had the highest divorce rate in the world (Lovett 2007). Increasing numbers of women were entering the public sphere through work, education, and civic activities. The shifting roles of women, along with declining birthrates among the white population of Northern European descent contributed to fears that both motherhood and the "American race" were eroding. In a turn toward what historian Laura Lovett calls, "nostalgic modernism," reformers seized on idealized images of the white rural family of the past as the model for social change. She explains, "Building on a Jeffersonian tradition of agrarianism, these reformers promoted similar variants of a highly idealized vision of the 'hearty, pioneer family' made strong, physically and morally, by their efforts to settle on and make their living from the land" (Lovett 2007). The myth of agrarianism, harnessed in the service of rural reform efforts, therefore gained increased salience and significance, not despite, but because the actual lived experiences of farmers and their families increasingly failed to conform to it. Strengthening rural families became a matter of national preservation, and the myth of agrarianism an "ideological instrument of perceived progress" at the same time that it served as a justification for the circumstances of those who stayed in rural areas, even as the realities of farm life were making it increasingly difficult to sustain (Lovett 2007).

Combined with agrarianism, ideological processes assigning meaning to gender also provided important conditions of existence for the hybrid family farm. In fact, agrarianism itself was a gendered ideology, prescribing different roles for men and women on the farm, and establishing a hierarchy between them. Fink discusses the gendered manifestations of agrarian ideology in depth, beginning with Jefferson's formulation. She demonstrates how Jefferson's agrarian vision of a land of free and independent producers was a vision for (some) men only. She explains how Jefferson's writings about farm women, though sparse, demonstrate that "[h]is agrarian vision hinged on the subordination of women. Women were not farmers. ... White women were the daughters, wives, and mothers of men, and their fulfillment came from comforting and supporting men within the family" (Fink 1992, 20). The ideal agrarian society hinged on the notion of separate spheres for men and women, with women relegated to the household and men to the farm enterprise. Hence, the prescription for the traditional feudal family was a fundamental component of agrarianism.

Gendered agrarianism helped to disguise women's work inside the farm household because their work was seen as part of a natural order – what women do, or were supposed to do. In his preface to the 1909 report on the problems of country life, President Roosevelt expressed this sentiment. "If the woman shirks her duty as housewife, as home keeper, as the mother whose prime function it is to bear and rear a sufficient number of healthy children, then she is not entitled to our regard" (Country Life Commission 1917, 9).

Even though farm women did much of the work of "farming" in the family farm enterprise – gardening, milking, and caring for chickens, for example – farm women were never considered to be "farmers" themselves. Even their labor in commercial farm production was described as "helping out." Men were the "real" farmers. Farm women also often sold their products for cash. This income played an important role in supporting the farm family. Yet, farm women's work was viewed as having saved money instead of having earned it. Even though they were often the primary breadwinners for the family, farm women were not recognized as such.

Agrarianism also helped elevate the masculine work of farming over the feminine work of home-making and the ancient class process over the feudal. A common saying of the time was, "A barn can build a house sooner than a house can build a barn." This statement expresses the perception that expenditures for the farm household were unproductive and wasteful, while expenditures for the farm enterprise were productive and profitable. Economic "rationality" required that limited resources be devoted to the commercial farm enterprise as the "real" source of income and the economic heart of the farm family. Even contemporary authors whose work is aimed at recovering the contributions of farm women in preserving the family farm maintain the perception that economic activity and production was confined to the farm enterprise and, in particular, to the work of the ancient farmer. According to Kleinegger, the "hardheaded reality" was that "in their quest for modern conveniences farm women had to struggle against a compelling economic imperative requiring that limited resources be reinvested in the farm ... because that was where the income was" (Kleinegger 1988, 175). She continues, discussing how purchases of household appliances reflect farm women's role as consumers, ignoring both that production occurred in the household, and that such production often generated substantial income for the farm family.

A further implication is that sacrifice would be necessary, but temporary, and belt-tightening for the sake of the farm enterprise would pay off later with bigger houses as well as bigger barns. The rhetoric and perception of economic imperative and sacrifice is similar to the argument often presented to workers in capitalist enterprises today. Accept lower wages, longer hours, and fewer benefits for the sake of saving the business. Workers' sacrifice is presented as the only and best option, and workers' wages are presented as an unreasonable drain on profits. Workers' roles in producing value and in generating those profits is de-emphasized.

Many farm wives, however, discovered that the new barn was all they got. Consider the following excerpt from the 1909 article on Mattie Corson's survey:

> Three-fourths of the girls said that they did not want a farmer for a husband, because – and this answer was general – they had seen how, their mothers slaved from dawn and before dawn, to night: and they had seen – and this was significant – they had seen all too plainly how their fathers think of nothing but their cattle and crops, to the sacrifice of their wives. The cattle must have everything: Mother nothing.
>
> (*The Ladies' Home Journal* 1909)

The needs of the ancient class process took precedence over the needs of the feudal. The seasonality of men's work in the fields may partially explain why such work took precedence over women's work in household production. Yet, even when seasonal demands overlapped, the production of cash crops took precedence over home production. Women could not ignore the labor of men, whether they were engaging in it or not, because their work could be disrupted at any time with a call to help in the field. In addition, women had to adjust their work to accommodate the needs of the ancient farmer and his workers, by adjusting meal preparation times, for example, or providing meals and rooms for hired hands. Neth (1998) found that farm men rarely took note of women's weekly or daily production activities, and mentioned these only when they impinged on their own work. Women's work was therefore, largely "invisible to the men of the farm" (Neth 1998, 27). And because women's work in childcare and food preparation was ongoing and continual, while men's work was seasonal, farm men enjoyed periods of relatively free time during which they could pursue leisure or civic activities that further enhanced their status in the community.

It was perfectly acceptable, even desirable, for women to perform masculine tasks when necessary, but the opposite was not true. Recall that many farm girls did farm work, but very few farm boys did housework. As the oldest child, one Iowa farm woman recalled being her "Dad's chore boy," driving horses, disking, and putting up hay (Neth 1998, 25). When women and girls stepped into the role of laborers in commercial farm production, they did so in spite of their female sex. They were allowed to assume a masculine role only because an appropriate male to perform the required work was unavailable or unaffordable. In doing so, they did not necessarily challenge the gender processes that defined the role as masculine, nor did they contribute to an increased recognition of the value of feminine work. More prosperous, and "progressive," farmers could afford to save their feminine hands for "feminine" work, and thus maintained a stricter division of labor between enterprise and household (Neth 1998, 25, 279). Boys who took on household tasks when women and girls were unavailable often felt inferior and "usually chafed at the lowered status" (Neth 1998, 27).

During the early decades of the twentieth century, agrarianism was also a racialized ideology, its gendered implications combined with a unique form of nationalistic pronatalism (Casey 2004; Lovett 2007). Farm women and children were at the center of these efforts. Notions of domesticity exalted motherhood as the natural and instinctive role of all women. Womanhood was equated with motherhood. Pronatalism was "coercive" in the sense that "the decision not to reproduce was not presented ... as a reasonable alternative" (Lovett 2007). This "coercive pronatalism" was codified, for example, in the 1873 Comstock Law, a federal statute that outlawed the distribution of birth control devices or informa-tion, among other "obscene" material, until the contraceptive ban was overturned in 1936 (Fink 1992). However, declining birthrates among white, urban women challenged this ideal. One editorial in *The Farmer's Wife* reflected these con-cerns that urban women were "shirking responsibility at every turn," having "given up their jobs as homemakers," while "the farm women of America, God bless them!, continue to live in the way that the normal wife and the normal mother should live." American farm women were "saving the ideals of home life" (*The Farmer's Wife* 1920; Casey 2004). The early twentieth century there-fore saw a unique marriage of pronatalism with agrarianism tinged with a eugenic ideal of race betterment. The overlap between the agrarian and maternal was reflected, for example, in the use of the numerous metaphors for farm women's roles which appeared in *The Farmer's Wife*, and played on the double meanings of notions such as fertility, nurturing, sowing, reaping, and growing. Farm women were represented as "tillers of familial soil," and "raising a crop of moral citizens." Farm children were referred to as their "domestic" or "child crop" (Casey 2004).

The family farm was viewed as the ideal place to raise children and to incul-cate them with the values of autonomy, nobility, virtue, and thrift. Farm children were viewed as national assets. According to rural sociologist, Josiah Galpin, the social role of farm children was in carrying the "stamina of the race," as "the contribution of rural life to the human stock of society" (Galpin 1918). Teddy Roosevelt popularized the term "race suicide" to express that idea that women who did not fulfill their roles as mothers endangered not only themselves and their families, but also the fate of the nation as a whole (Fink 1992). The "race" of concern was that of the white, "native-born" population, or those of mostly Northern European descent. As representatives of this "Americanness" white farm families were seen as the ideal, authentic embodiments of American virtue and character. Racialized agrarianism, therefore, elevated the role of farm mothers in producing and reproducing future farmers and their wives to a matter of "race preservation."

This confluence of ideologies provided conditions of existence for the hybrid family farm, and the continued feudal exploitation of farm women and their children. The notion that motherhood was a woman's natural role served to disguise the difficult work of childbearing and rearing, particularly under the conditions of rural life at the time. Ideals of motherhood identified the interests of children with that of their mothers, hiding the conflict between a farm woman's role as both nurturer and exploiter (or enabler of the exploitation) of her children, thereby enabling children's serfdom. Farm women's own dependency and exploitation was reproduced, as well, through emotional ties and obligation to their children. Nationalistic ideas of race betterment further reinforced the virtue of farm women's motherly sacrifice in the service of a greater good. In this way, the benefits of farm women's labor as mothers accrued to society at large, while the costs of childbearing and childrearing were extracted privately from women within the farm family (Fink 1992).

A central component of the agrarian vision is a celebration of rugged individualism, independence, and self-reliance. Yet it is not a vision of an individual farmer, but of an individual farm family. Like other aspects of agrarianism, this one was gendered, and had contradictory implications for the family farm's class structures. Farm families were deemed independent and self-reliant in relation to the outside world, but inside the family farm isolation meant the farm family had to be a cohesive, interdependent unit. Whereas farm families were representatives of democracy to the outside world, inside they were autocratic and ruled by the farmer as head of household. Any displays of individualism and independence on the part of women and children were actively, and sometimes violently, discouraged as a threat to family cohesiveness and therefore to the survival of the family farm. As the rural historian David Danbom (1979) explains, "It seems, therefore, that individualism, a rural trait both praised and damned by outside observers, was enjoyed by adult males only."

This privileged access to agency, democracy, and independence was reinforced by legal structures and customs that gave adult males power to command the vital economic resource of land. In most cases, women and children had access to land only through their feudal relationships to men. Studies of inheritance patterns show that male children received land while female children received movable goods, education, or cash (Fink 1992, 124; Friedberger 1983). Even when women brought their own land to the marriage and retained title to it, custom gave the authority to decide its use to the husband. Political processes thereby assigned power over the land on which both the farm enterprise and farm household resided to the husband, providing a condition of existence for both the feudal and ancient class processes. In addition, of course, was the fact that many women lacked the legal right to vote during the early part of this period, and therefore lacked the recognition of their democratic rights as citizens.

The isolation that came with the relative self-sufficiency and emphasis on hard work and personal responsibility insulated the farm family, and in particular farm women, from economic and social contact with the outside world. This lack of contact reduced their exposure to alternative ideas and models of living that would have led them to question their own life circumstances. There were not many acceptable alternatives in employment for adult women in rural areas. This lack of opportunity was compounded by the lack of time, education, access to loans, land, or authority that would have allowed them to surmount the feudal, exploitative relationship in family farming. Farm women lacked time and social networks, and were isolated geographically, economically, and socially. Their work rarely took them off the farm as that of men did, and even though many farm households had access to modern communication and transportation technologies like telephones and automobiles, women did not necessarily have access to these items without their husband's approval or accompaniment (Jellison 1993). The isolation of farm women and children provided conditions of existence for their feudal dependency, and ensured that the ancient farmer could avail himself of a captive, cheap labor force that was unlikely to be able to bargain for increased pay or better working conditions because they were tied to their ancient hybrid employer through familial obligations.

The demands of hard work, as well as rural isolation and agrarian pride, were reinforced by rural institutions including the church, the school, the neighborhood, and the family itself. Most farm people lived the way they had been raised, as prescribed by their churches, schooling, neighbors, and family. The bonds of feudal obligation were sealed with the marriage contract and a woman's entry into the role of farm wife. All of these conditions combined to entrap farm women, and also farm men, into their respective roles in the feudal class structure. These same conditions, with their gendered impacts, combined to produce and reproduce the ancient class process as well as the farmer in his role within it. Finally, these conditions shaped the primacy of the ancient class structure over the feudal, as well as the transfer of resources from the latter in order to subsidize the survival of the former.

The combination of ideological, political, economic, and other conditions of existence supporting the family farm hybrid also pushed and pulled it in contradictory directions, which served to undermine it as well. The isolation that insulated farm families also increased the psychological and economic stresses associated with reproducing the feudal and ancient class structures. Agrarian mythology which celebrated rural living contributed to the appalling conditions there in part because it served to gloss them over. The increased concern for rural backwardness coming from the Country Life Movement was driven not only by this ideology, but also by the recognition of the gaping chasm between the beloved ideal and the actual conditions. Attention to the problems of rural life served to increase awareness of the situation, and gave farm women and others a voice to express their discontent and to read about the discontent of others. Because neither reformers nor farm families were aware of the class dimensions of their problems, the solutions they proposed and adopted failed to address them. Faced with the intractable problems of rural life, increasing numbers of farm men, and especially women and children, fled farm life altogether.

Feudal-ancient subsidies: making do and helping out

As the preceding discussion indicates, farm women and children performed a variety of labor processes within the feudal class structure of the family farm – both in farm and household production. These labor processes subsidized the family farm enterprise's ancient, or ancient-feudal, hybrid class structure in two ways. First, they resulted in services, products, and proceeds to meet the needs of farm family members, called "making do." Second, they supplemented the ancient farmer's surplus in the production of commercial farm commodities, called "helping out." The work of farm women, with the aid of their children, provided substantially for the reproduction of the farm family and, in so doing, provided an important source of subsidy to the family farm's ancient class structure, enabling it to survive and prosper, even as the burden of work was shifted thus onto the shoulders of the feudal serfs – farm wives and their children. As Bailey (1915, 348) noted in her analysis of the 1912 survey of farm homes, the income from the "minor farm enterprises, such as the poultry, the garden, the orchard, and the dairy," along with the "unpaid labor of the family *make the returns of the farm business a profit instead of a loss*" (emphasis added). It was the work of feudal serfs that played a significant role in purchasing the "self-sufficiency" of farm families, and insulated them from the uncertainties of the farm enterprise income. In this section, I examine the value connections between the family farm's feudal and ancient class structures by rethinking the important practices of "making do" and "helping out" in these terms.

Making do

Women substituted their own labor in household production in order to save on cash expenditures. "Making do" or "saving money through the use of labor or simply doing without" was often used to describe what farm women did, or were supposed to do (Neth 1998, 9). The turn of the twentieth century equivalent of "reduce, reuse, recycle," making do was a valued and celebrated skill, "the measure of a good wife," according to one farm woman (Neth 1998, 31). Those who were not so talented were subject not only to denigrating gossip, but the possibility of failure during hard times when "making do" was crucial for the family farm's survival. Popular farm women's magazines like *The Farmer's Wife* frequently published advice about how to make do, or economize, in order to reduce expenditure.

In class terms, making do was a strategy to shape the flow of surplus between the feudal and ancient class structures of the family farm. Specifically, making do meant that surplus produced and appropriated within the feudal class process was diverted to that of the ancient, and therefore unavailable to secure the necessary feudal conditions of existence. It was a transfer of surplus produced by the farm wife, appropriated by her husband in his position as feudal lord, and then transferred to the ancient farm enterprise by virtue of his position as ancient producer and appropriator. Making do operated to shift surplus from the feudal class structure to ancient farm production as needed, to facilitate expansion during times of prosperity or survival during times of crisis. The transfer of surplus to the ancient from the feudal class structures in family farms is analogous to the transfer of goods and services to children in the form of childcare in contemporary feudal households (Resnick and Wolff 2009). Just as the husband transfers his wife's appropriated surplus to children in various concrete forms in order to facilitate their survival and growth, the farm husband transferred his wife's appropriated surplus to the ancient farm enterprise in various concrete forms in order to facilitate its survival and growth. The farm wife's feudal exploitation, therefore, enabled and helped reproduce the ancient farmer's own auto-exploitation.

The transfer of surplus from feudal to ancient meant that the ancient farmer's consumption no longer depended solely on his necessary labor. Expenditures from the feudal class structure subsidized the farmer/husband's personal consumption. This subsidy was a transfer of surplus – in kind or in cash – produced by the farm wife, appropriated by her husband in his position as feudal lord, and then transferred to his consumption as ancient farmer. The farmer used these expenditures from the feudal class structure to reproduce his ancient labor power for work in the family farm enterprise.

The subtractions from the feudal surplus flowing into the subsidy were made available as a non-class revenue flow to the ancient farmer's personal consumption. What the feudal class structure lost was gained by the ancient farmer. This subsidy supplemented the ancient farmer's necessary labor, the total value of the goods and services the ancient farmer had to consume to reproduce his labor power at the prevailing social standard. If children or hired hands were helping out in the production of ancient farm commodities (rendering them ancient/feudal/capitalist hybrid farm commodities), the subsidy would consist of the sum of the multiple transfers from the farm wife to support, as well, the personal consumption of these serfs and other workers.

Transfers from the feudal class structure might have been offset by outlays from the ancient farmer to the feudal class structure, a transfer of value between the ancient and the feudal class structures via the farmer/husband, because he occupied two different class positions. While the feudal farm wife's making do subsidized the ancient farmer's personal consumption, this theoretically may have enabled him, in turn, to redirect a portion of his necessary labor, or the "wage" he paid himself for self-exploitation, back to his wife (and children). This transfer may have taken a monetary form of proceeds from the sale of crops, or a non-monetary form of actual farm produce like portions of grain to feed dairy cows and chickens, or beef from the production of livestock. It therefore constituted a portion of the farmer's ancient necessary labor, which he diverted from his own consumption in reproducing the labor power he expended in the production of ancient, or ancient/feudal, hybrid farm commodities, to the feudal class structure. This transfer was made available to the feudal class structure in the form of non-class revenue to finance the outlays required for its reproduction. As above, if the labor of the ancient farmer was supplemented by feudal or other kinds of workers in the family farm enterprise, the total non-class revenue would become the sum of the multiple transfers to the feudal class structure from each individual worker's necessary labor.

While it may be the case that what was given up by the feudal (ancient) class structure in providing the transfer to the ancient (feudal) was exactly offset by what was gained, there was no necessity for this equality to hold, and every reason to believe that it often did not. It is likely that the ancient subsidy to the feudal class structure was smaller than the feudal subsidy to the ancient, as the strategy of making do operated to shift surplus from the feudal class structure to the ancient as needed to facilitate expansion during times of prosperity, or survival during times of crisis.[12]

Farm women's work in making do helped meet the consumption needs of the farm family, thereby allowing for the production of a larger ancient surplus in the production of farm commodities. The high value placed on the practice of making do, and its importance in farm women's identity, probably contributed toward reducing ancient transfers to the feudal class structure at any given time, and particularly in times of crisis for the ancient class process in the family farm enterprise. As discussed above, the services, products, and income generated by farm women's work met the majority of the needs of the farm family, and often much more, with little contribution from the ancient farm enterprise revenues or the ancient farmer himself. It seems likely that many farms experienced a situation in which the diversion of the farm wife's surplus to subsidize her husband's consumption as a farmer was not offset by an equal infusion from ancient necessary labor. Making do was therefore an important strategy in overdetermining the family farm's hybrid class structure. By subsidizing her husband's consumption, a farm wife's labor enabled a lower ancient necessary labor for a given level of ancient consumption. The feudal subsidy in effect allowed the ancient farmer to pay himself a lower wage, or even none at all if the subsidy was sufficient. In turn, this lowered ancient necessary labor enabled a higher ancient surplus in ancient farm enterprise production, and hence a rising ancient rate of class exploitation, or the ratio of ancient surplus to ancient necessary labor. The expanded ancient surplus allowed the ancient class structure in the family farm enterprise to access expanded conditions of existence.[13]

Family farmers' willingness to tolerate intense rates of self-exploitation is widely recognized (although not in those terms) as an important contributor to the conundrum of family farm survival. Whether it is called "the distinct calculus of the family farm" or "the peasant mode of production," the role of farm women's exploitation in enabling this survival is important to recognize. (See Reinhardt and Bartlett (1989) for a review of this literature.)

While the increased ancient surplus became an important component of the survival of the farm enterprise, it simultaneously threatened the reproduction of the feudal class structure by diverting the feudal surplus available to secure its conditions of existence, without an offsetting infusion from the ancient farmer's necessary labor. One widespread response, or set of responses, was to reduce the outlays necessary for feudal subsumed class payments by reducing either the number of conditions of existence or their price.

The latter was accomplished as farm wives themselves often took on the responsibility of managing, supervising, and keeping accounts of their own surplus production. For example, Mrs. E.G.R. (1924) quoted above was responsible for handling the "whole family pocketbook," and had been managing the family's income for over thirty years without supervision (except her own). She explained that in spite of her decision-making authority over family finances, she almost never spent the money on herself. Thirty-two percent of women reported managing farm accounts and 30 percent home accounts in the Ward survey. Twenty-nine percent kept dairy records, and 45 percent poultry records. Ward explains that these women recognized the importance of "getting the most from a dollar and making sure that the home industry pays." With or without compensation for their services, farm women, then, commonly occupied subsumed class positions enabling their own continued exploitation in farm and household production by supervising and managing family farm value flows. The Smith Lever Act of 1914 provided funding for USDA home demonstration agents to teach and encourage the spread of such farm home management practices, thus encouraging farm wives to take an even more active and explicit role in managing the extraction of their own surplus. Women's role in making such management decisions does not in any way undermine the exploitative feudal class process in which they participated. On the contrary, it served as one of its conditions of existence. These women wielded some command over value flows, and used their power over those flows to reproduce their own serfdom. That farm women often performed these functions without expecting or receiving compensation further strengthened the family farm's exploitative feudal class structure by reducing subsumed class payments to reproduce this condition of its existence, thus helping to offset the inequality in the feudal budget.

A second method of reducing feudal subsumed class payments was to curtail the number of conditions of existence – to stop paying for one or several of them temporarily or permanently. In fact, reducing feudal subsumed class payments for new feudal means of production, especially for farm household production, was an important component of family farm reproduction. Farm women did not typically have access to the same labor-saving conveniences that urban women did. Most urban homes had indoor plumbing, hot running water, central heating, electricity, and telephones, which, as noted above, most rural homes did not. Urban women also had access to a plethora of labor-saving implements for household production, including power washing machines, electric irons, ranges, and vacuums. In addition, urban women could purchase many of the products like clothing and food that farm women still produced at home (Knowles 1988, 313). In fact, with the exception of the sewing machine, farm women's means of production remained little changed from that of their mothers and even their grandmothers (Knowles 1988, 307).

Some of this discrepancy was undoubtedly due to the underdeveloped rural infrastructure or isolation, making some goods and services prohibitively expensive or simply unavailable in many rural areas. Some of the difference, however, cannot be explained by expense or availability, as many farm homes lacked what the farm enterprise did not. According to the Ward survey, for example, 48 percent of the farms had power to operate farm machinery, but only 22 percent had power in the farm home (Ward 1920, 442). This inequality between expenditures on new, labor-saving means of production and equipment in the farm home and in the farm enterprise was widely remarked upon. A 1915 sociology textbook noted, "Money is freely spent, when new machinery is needed on the farm, or another fifty-acre piece is added after a prosperous season, but seldom a thought to the needs of the kitchen" (Kleinegger 1988, 172–173). As Jane Knowles (1988, 314) acknowledged in her study of farm women's activism between 1900 and 1920, "Rural women clearly were disadvantaged in the material conditions of their daily working lives vis-à-vis both rural men and urban women."

Even though opportunities for increasing farm women's relative surplus product through productivity-improving feudal means of production were limited, production of feudal absolute surplus remained high, and probably expanded as needed. This was another possible response to the inequality in the feudal budget due to the transfers required for the farmer husband's consumption. Farm wives' responsibilities were formulated in terms of tasks completed, rather than time spent. Washing, mending, and meals had to be accomplished on a daily or weekly basis, no matter how arduous or time-consuming the tasks. This piecework character of farm women's tasks helped maintain, if not increase, their production of feudal surplus. Another source of feudal surplus was additional serfs, as discussed above. Young children and older girls often helped their mothers in the production of feudal surplus.

Making do meant balancing and managing the needs of the family farm's complex and connected class structures. Increasing the feudal surplus labor and reducing feudal subsumed class payments helped offset the net expenditures needed to subsidize the ancient farmer's consumption. The farm wife's strategy of making do, as well as the addition of the feudal surplus labor of her children may well have succeeded in balancing the feudal class budget. Even so, there was no guarantee that the equality between revenues and expenditures could hold indefinitely, or that the balance signified the long term viability of the feudal class structure. Indeed, the strategy of making do had contradictory implications for its continuing viability as a survival strategy, as it meant that farm women shouldered a heavy burden of long hours and backbreaking work. These were among the conditions contributing most to the "farm woman problem" and pushing women and girls from rural areas.[14]

Helping out

While the work of farm women (and children) and the feudal surplus they produced provided for most, if not all, of the consumption needs of the ancient farmer, thereby allowing him to increase the time during which he produced surplus, the physical labor requirements of the field crop and livestock operation at times swelled beyond his own means of meeting them, as indicated in Figure 2.2. At these times, it was necessary to supplement the strategy of making do with the additional strategy of helping out. In addition to their household, barn, and garden duties, farm women and children also "helped out" in commercial farm production – most commonly those tasks related to the production of livestock like beef cattle and hogs, and field crops like corn and wheat. Examples of helping out tasks, as previously discussed, included driving horses for plowing or disking, putting up hay, shocking wheat, picking corn, or driving the tractor (Neth 1998, 45).

Like the strategy of making do, helping out had the contradictory impact of resolving a potential crisis for the ancient class structure by displacing it onto the feudal class structure, in turn impacting on the long term viability of these strategies and the ancient class structure depending upon them. In the section that follows, I present the class analysis and ramifications of helping out.

As discussed above, surveys found that many women helped with field work for several weeks out of the year. Poverty, hired labor shortages, or lack of suitable male feudal helpers could force women into the fields at crucial times of the year. This labor was usually contingent and irregular, although for some women it was not. Being able to save farm women's labor power for "women's work" was a badge of status, as farmers sought to emulate the urban middle class lifestyle associated with the male breadwinner-female caretaker model of the household. Wealthier, "progressive" farmers – those who could afford to adopt the cutting edge new agricultural production methods – could purchase their wives' freedom from the drudgery of helping out in order to conform, or to appear to conform, more closely to the urban ideal of the cult of domesticity. Advertisements and other media, educational texts, and religious messages shaped farm men and women's aspirations of mimicking the urban, middle class, white households in which women were seen as leisurely housewives, consuming and not producing, within the home. Just as housewives who did not work outside the home for wages were associated with higher income and status for their husbands, farm wives who did not work outside in the farm fields were associated with higher income and status for their farmer husbands, even if changing the mere geography of farm women's work did not actually reduce their workload. Not only could more prosperous farmers afford to replace female field workers with hired hands and machines, they also had larger farms, which meant longer distances between the fields and the farmhouse, and hence greater physical separation between the feudal worksite in the home and its environs, and the ancient worksite in the fields and pastures.[15] Mary Neth's analysis of Midwestern farm women's oral histories is a case in point. She found that those on smaller farms (80 acres or less) were the most active in the barnyard and fields, while those on the largest farms (240 acres or more) were the least active (Neth 1998, 567).

Given the requirements of "making do" (along with the fact that the most onerous requirements for helping out probably coincided with the busy summer and fall months when making do also required more time for gathering, butchering, picking, canning, and drying of products associated with the farm wife's barnyard, garden, and household work) it would have been next to impossible for most farm women to add still additional work in the fields except for emergencies. If a farm wife were spending time working in the fields or tending to livestock, who did the cooking, washing, carrying water, cleaning the lamps, tending the children, planting garden produce, feeding the chickens, milking the cows, ironing, mending, sweeping, or baking? In short, how did all of her other tasks get accomplished?

In addition, the presence of young children would have served to constrain farm women's work in the fields unless they were able to take their children with them, especially since farm women received little help either from older children or their husbands with childcare. High birthrates in rural areas prevented many women from straying too far from the house to do field work. The story of "Mrs. Green," a Kansas farm woman interviewed by Children's Bureau researchers as part of a study of rural maternal and infant care, illustrates the challenges many farm women faced. Mrs. Green had four living children, ranging in age from 15 months to 10 years. While as a girl she "drove teams" and "helped with the outdoor chores" in addition to helping with the housework, as an adult she did no outdoor work except for caring for the chickens. During harvest times, she had to cook for extra men, in addition to juggling all of her usual duties. When the youngest child was nine months old, Mrs. Green "could get no help at harvest." Consequently, "it was then that the baby got diarrhea because she was unable to watch what he ate" (Moore, E. 1917).

As discussed above, it was mostly the older boys who helped out with ancient commercial farm production, working alongside their fathers in the role of farmer serf-apprentices. Their work was often supplemented by the help of older girls. The discussion that follows, therefore, focuses on the work of farm children in helping out, but it should be kept in mind that the discussion also applies to those many farm women who also did this work and added to their already onerous duties in the farm household, barnyard, and garden. As Carolyn Sachs writes in her history of women's agricultural labor, "women have always worked in the fields during periods of labor shortage, but rarely has their domestic workload decreased in relation to their involvement in field work" (Sachs 1983, 13).

In addition, the possibility of hired hands is considered, as their labor was also employed to supplement that of the ancient farmer, and their presence also impacted upon farm women's work. Figure 2.7 shows total farm employment, as well as the shares held by unpaid and hired workers, and indicates the greater significance of unpaid workers in total farm employment.

Helping out meant that the unpaid feudal surplus labor of family members was added to the farmer's ancient surplus labor, and ancient farm commodities became hybrid farm commodities. I use the term helping out because this was the phrase commonly used to signify this type of work whenever it was not the ancient farmer doing it. In this way, the vocabulary preserved the ancient farmer's identity as the "real" farmer, even though he relied upon the labor of others on a regular basis. Helping out was analogous to the medieval European system

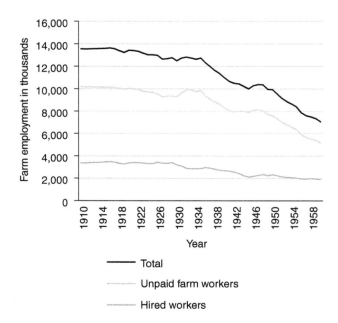

Figure 2.7 Farm employment, 1910–1960 (data from Carter, Susan B., Scott Sigmund Gartner, Michael R. Haines, Alan L. Olmstead, Richard Sutch, and Gavin Wright, ed. 2006. *Historical Statistics of the United States, Earliest Times to the Present: Millennial Edition Online*. New York: Cambridge University Press. Available online at http://hsus.cambridge.org/HSUSWeb/ HSUSEntryServlet).

of corvée, in which serfs joined a team of workers on the lord's lands either for a fixed number of days each season, or for assisting in a definite task until it was complete (Duby 1968).

Helping out was a strategy to promote the short term survival and long term reproduction of family farm ancient class processes. As previously discussed, farm children constituted a reserve army of labor that could be called upon as needed during crucial harvesting or planting times when the work requirements of the ancient farm enterprise swelled beyond the ability of the ancient farmer to accomplish them alone, and when he required the help of his male apprentices and other farm family members. Children's labor was a crucial factor in the success of family farms. Studies of census data and family farm survival rates show a distinct correlation between the number of children and a farm family's standard of living (Kirkpatrick 1929). Fink found in her study of Nebraska farms that of the families containing married women between the ages of 35 and 44 in 1900, those that were present in the 1910 census had an average of 6.3 surviving children as opposed to those that did not, with an average of 4.7. She did not find the same correlation with the presence of hired hands (Fink 1992, 148). The significance and impact of helping out by farm children is evidenced, for example, by the differences in the application of child labor and compulsory education laws to rural versus urban children. The length of the school years differed as well. In rural areas, children's schooling was arranged around harvesting and planting times, with the result that they got less of it. For example, in 1910, the average rural school year was 137.7 days, compared to the urban average of 184.3 days (Danbom 1979).

As they were meant to eventually become ancient farmers themselves through inheritance, marriage, or purchase, farmer serf-apprentices ensured the long term reproduction of the ancient farm enterprise. The unpaid labor of farm family members saved on expenses for hired field hands, particularly during those times when help was in high demand and therefore more expensive. The child labor force was not only cheaper but also easier to discipline than hired workers, and this contributed to farm families' reliance on their labor (Fink 1992, 148). Hybridization of this type of farm production through helping out thus provided an important condition of existence for the family farm ancient class process by increasing the surplus available to meet its conditions of existence.

In class terms, child serfs and farmer serf-apprentices performed feudal surplus labor alongside the ancient farmer, producing a class structural hybrid in commercial farm production (contained within the hybrid of the family farm enterprise, within the hybrid of the family farm). The commodity produced was a hybrid commodity because the labor processes occurred along with the ancient and feudal class processes at the same time.[16] While feudal surplus labor was added to that of the ancient to supplement revenues, the formation of the helping out hybrid required no further subsumed class payments to reproduce it. Helping out was merely an extension of existing family farm feudal class processes to different types of labor processes. Likewise, ancient subsumed class payments were neither increased nor decreased with the helping out hybrid.[17]

"Helping out" increased the surplus available to the ancient farmer, allowing him to access expanded conditions of existence. This probably added to the burden on farm women because of the increased demands of "making do" to subsidize the consumption of the ancient-feudal hybrid farm enterprise work force, including the work of reproducing and caring for young children. In 1900, there were about 800 farm children under 5 years of age for every 1,000 rural women. This was twice the number that urban women had. The average household size was 5.2, and this number did not begin to decline significantly until after World War II (Gardner 2006). A farm woman's children might have helped ease the psychological strains of loneliness and isolation, while also freeing her from the demands of helping out in commercial farm production. At the same time, children added to her burden with other kinds of work and demands on her feudal surplus. Thus, help for the ancient farmer in the family farm enterprise produced the contradictory results of both enhancing and undermining his wife's feudal existence, and therefore his own as ancient farmer (Resnick and Wolff 2009).

In addition to unpaid feudal serfs, ancient farmers may have employed hired hands to help out. Hired hands came mostly from a neighborhood pool of less prosperous farmers, tenants, or landless laborers, including teenage sons. Like hired girls, hired hands might have labored as part of a neighborhood work exchange of ancients or feudal serf-apprentices. In addition, hired workers might have been part of a crew hired for a specific service, or custom work, like threshing, for example. In this case, their employer, not the farmer purchasing the custom services, would have been the appropriator and distributor of any surplus these workers produced.

Aside from these examples, hired hands probably labored for the farmer as his capitalist wage workers. One indicator that hired hands were specifically differentiated from feudal serfs, and therefore laboring in the context of a different form of relationship to their farmer employer, was the concern expressed by some farm women with housing and feeding these "outsiders" among the farm family. Another is the concern with potential shortages of hired laborers caused by their mobility – geographical or socioeconomic – and the fact that hired hands were likely to be more expensive. These examples point to the absence of the dependency and feudal obligation that would provide a condition of existence for feudal class processes to occur with hired hands' wage labor. Hence, while farm families sometimes employed a hired hand all year, or employed the same hired hands each season to ensure consistent quantity and quality of help, this would not necessarily be inconsistent with a capitalist wage relationship.

Capitalist wage workers would have established a new source of surplus labor in hybrid farm production. I confine the discussion that follows to the case of capitalist hired hands who were not part of established networks of feudal neighborhood workers, since feudal farmer-apprentices were included in the discussion above. The presence of hired hands necessitated further adjustments that did not necessarily reduce farm women's transfer of surplus labor, but merely changed the form in which surplus was delivered. Hired hands were paid in room and board, cash, or some combination of these (Garkovich and Bokemeier 1988, 217). Farm women did the work of meal preparation, cleaning, washing, and even sewing clothing for the non-cash component of hired hands' wages. Just as they did for feudal farmer serf-apprentices, farm wives subsidized a portion of hired hands' necessary labor, thus reducing the capitalist wage paid to them and increasing the surplus available to the ancient farmer. This subsidy was analogous to the ancient subsidy discussed above as the "making do" strategy. That hired hands placed an onerous burden on many farm women is evidenced by the fact that many "chose" to do field work themselves, rather than endure the intrusion of a hired man into their family lives, along with all of the work his presence entailed (Vanek 1980, 425). Thus, while hired hands reduced "men's work" for women, they did not necessarily reduce their overall workload, but merely changed its geography.

Help for farmers meant more work for farm wives. One Missouri wife lamented in the 1915 USDA survey, "Everyone is urging the farmer to raise crops. Now, all this means extra help for the woman to cook for, since all these crops have to be attended, harvested, and marketed" (USDA 1915). Comparing hired hands with other types of wage workers, one Nebraska farm woman suggested that the hired hand should "furnish his own dinner the same as the mason, carpenter, and painter, and all day laborers in the city" (USDA 1915, 50). One woman's letter to Secretary Houston in 1915 compares the farm wife's situation with that of the woman in town who takes in boarders. Her statement speaks to the differing conditions of rural and urban wives as they pertained to the class structures of family farms and the transfers of value between them:

> Men hearing of the town man marrying and having his wife take in from one to a dozen boarders, speak slightingly of the man, even though his wife is young and strong, with no family, and buys her eggs, butter, lard, vegetables, has her washing done, and handles at least part of the money received. The same men, if they happen to be farmers and their wives have several small children, will expect those wives to board from one to a dozen men, raise chickens, make butter, try out lard, help with the garden, and do their own washing, and handle no money for the extra labor.
>
> (*The New York Times* 1915)

The Ward survey found that on 80 percent of farms responding, five additional men were required for at least six weeks of the year (but recall that only 14 percent had hired help in the household). That the added burden weighed heavily on farm women is evident in their 1915 letters to Secretary Houston, many complaining bitterly of the extra work associated with hired farm help. The same woman quoted above described how "Serving hot, substantial meals at 6 o'clock a.m., 12 o'clock noon, and 6 o'clock p.m. and clearing up the dishes left no time for anything else," and declared that, "Each wife can 'strike'" (*The New York Times* 1915). Some women connected their troubles to the "so-called better farming, since it only meant more work for the whole family, with no real gain" (USDA 1915, 47). Thus, farm women noted how the move to bigger crops, larger farms (and more hired hands), was occurring at their expense. Mitchell's (1915) report on the letters sums up the situation:

> Abundant crops need hands to harvest them, and the farm woman must feed the hands. To many this is the last straw.... For them the labor problem is two edged. They can get no help themselves, and the help their husbands have they must care for.
>
> (Mitchell 1915)

Like making do, helping out meant balancing and managing the needs of the family farm's complex and interconnected class structures, always shaped by the primacy of the ancient class processes. Even if farm women were not helping out themselves in ancient/feudal hybrid commercial farm production, the increased surplus from feudal and capitalist workers merely transformed the farm wife's burden into the work of making do. As before, it is unlikely that the non-class revenue transfers from hybrid farm production to the feudal class structure were sufficient to offset the increased expenditures from the feudal surplus labor of the farm wife to subsidize hybrid farm production. One solution to the problems of helping out by feudal serfs or hired hands was that their labor could be replaced through the purchase of labor-saving machinery in hybrid farm production. This strategy, and its impact, is the subject of Chapter 3.

The combined demands of helping out and making do, as well as the extraordinary capacity of farm women to endure these circumstances, is illustrated in the story of one farm woman as recounted in a 1917 study of maternity and infant care in Kansas:

> On a 380-acre farm the baby was born in the latter part of May, the sixth child in a family whose eldest was only 8 years old.... [After two weeks, the mother] did all her regular work, including milking, gardening, and the care of chickens. Harvest came when the baby was 3 weeks old, bringing 5 "hands" for 2 weeks; at thrashing, immediately after harvest, 2 haulers were boarded for 2 days. The mother had no help with the housework during this time, but she did no milking or gardening through the harvest period; as far as possible she had "got her work done up ahead" the first week she was up from bed.
>
> (Moore, E. 1917)

The farm woman problem revisited

> The life of the farm woman is built on service. Through her busy days, with their multitude of homely tasks, she smooths the path of daily living for her family – whatever it is, no task is too humble, no sacrifice too great, if through it she smooths the path for someone else. They are the expression of the spirit of motherhood and 'neighborhood' that makes the pattern of her daily life.
>
> (*The Farmer's Wife* 1928)

The job of making do meant that farm women substituted their own labor in place of expenditures, by producing goods and services, or the proceeds from these, for the use of the farm family. During this period, the resulting long work hours were noted with concern in several studies and by farm women themselves. Ward identified the long workday, along with the preponderance of heavy manual labor as two of the "outstanding problems" of farm women.

The long hours of work were one factor constraining leisure and vacation time for farm women.[18] In the first Bailey (1915) study, several women reported an average of 3.5 hours per day for "personal" and "recreation" purposes, while "only two of the thirteen women had what might be termed a real vacation." Six were away from home for no longer than one day during the entire year. Women in the Michigan study reported an average of two hours of leisure time per day for the year. Nineteen of the 91 farm women reported having no leisure time during the summer months (Bailey and Snyder 1921). Likewise, 87 percent of the women in the Ward survey reported no vacation during the year. *The Literary Digest*, reporting on a 1919 survey of 1,400 farm women by the New York

State College of Agriculture at Cornell University found in their long hours and working conditions "Some Solid Reasons for a Strike of Farm-Wives" (1919). One Missouri farm woman wrote in response to the 1915 USDA survey of the wives of crop correspondents, "I have been a farmer's wife for thirty years and have never had a vacation" (*The New York Times* 1915). Another from Kansas noted that during eight months of the year, her workday averaged 16 hours, her husband's 15. "There are neighbors within two miles," she wrote, "nice people, that we haven't seen for five years" (*The New York Times* 1915).

The demands of making do during the busy summer months meant farm women worked longer days than in the winter, between two and three hours longer on average (Bailey and Snyder 1921; Bailey 1915; Ward 1920; Rankin 1928). Letters to the *Farmer's Wife* portray similar situations, as well as farm women's dissatisfaction with their double, or even triple shifts of farm and household work. "Out-of-Breath Betty" wrote in 1929,

> Is it really worthwhile to try to do the work of two or three women in a day? It is two or three, isn't it, when a woman does all the necessary work in a home and then helps her husband in the field, and raises a hundred chickens?

> (Kleinegger 1988, 170)

Figure 2.8, reproduced from Clark and Gray's 1927–1928 study of the "routine and seasonal work of Nebraska farm women," shows the seasonal fluctuations in farm women's work. Although no information on total time spent on each task is given, the chart does indicate the continuous burden of many tasks, such as milking and butter making, as well as the seasonal increase in tasks such as garden, chickens, and canning fruits and vegetables. Interestingly, farm women seem to have found some extra time during the busy summer months by reducing time spent on things like sewing and household chores.

Figure 2.9 shows the average number of extra meals served in each household per month (to both visitors and help) reported in the same study. The number was steady at about 17 per household through the winter and early spring, before springing up to an incredible 61 extra meals in July and 47 in August. As the authors note, the tremendous burden of these extra mouths to feed was all the more so because it came during the busiest months (Clark and Gray 1930).

Let us re-visualize the farm woman problem in class terms by examining the farm wife's 24-hour day. A significant portion of her day was devoted to feudal necessary and surplus labor time. Recall that making do often required that farm women spend an additional number of hours performing feudal and ancient subsumed class services of bookkeeping, managing, etc.

The remaining time she spent sleeping, relaxing, eating, etc. was her residual time. Using the data from the Rankin study, which seems to be representative, the first three components of a farm wife's day added up to about 12 hours in the summer and nine in winter. She spent about 7.5 and 9 hours asleep on average, summer and winter respectively, and 1.5 on meals. That left her residual time for

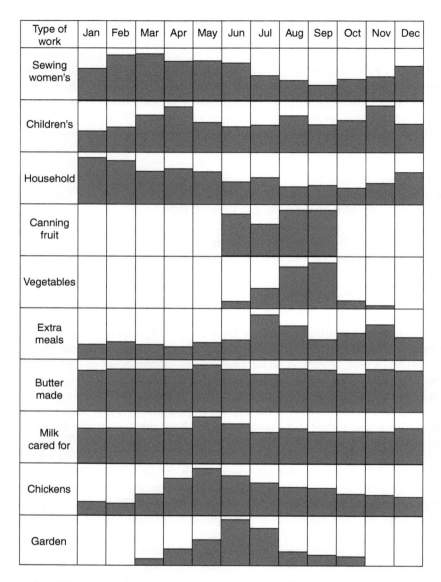

Figure 2.8 Seasonal demands on farm women's time (reprinted from Clark, Marjorie Ruth, and Greta Gray. 1930. "The Routine and Seasonal Work of Nebraska Farm Women." Bulletin University of Nebraska College of Agriculture 238: 5–39).

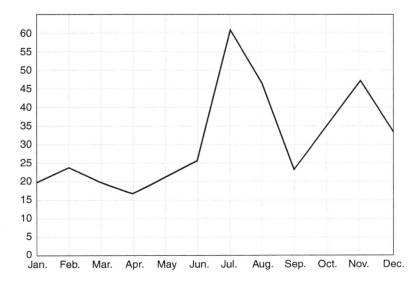

Figure 2.9 Average number of extra meals served in each household per month (reprinted from Clark, Marjorie Ruth, and Greta Gray. 1930. "The Routine and Seasonal Work of Nebraska Farm Women." Bulletin University of Nebraska College of Agriculture 238: 5–39).

leisure activities at only 3 hours per day in summer and 4.5 hours per day in winter on average (Rankin 1928, 5).[19]

These estimates clarify the extraordinary burden of making do for farm women, as well as the sacrifices it entailed. Just as the arrival of a child into the feudal household places added demands on a wife's time, so also did the necessity of supporting the ancient-hybrid farm enterprise and its workers. One of several adjustments was probably as indicated by the data. First, the demands of making do were met in part by increasing a farm woman's surplus labor, by simply adding additional tasks to those which she already performed. This adjustment increased working time and reduced leisure time, as the statistics on farm women's working hours indicate. With all that she had to do during the summer months, it is most likely that a farm woman's ability to stretch her surplus approached or surpassed her physical and emotional limitations. An alternative was to continue surplus labor as before, but simply reallocate it to more pressing tasks. Figure 2.8 indicates that farm women did this too, as discussed above. Finally, it seems that farm women also found the extra time they needed by reducing their own necessary labor and providing the difference as a gift to the ancient farmer and his workers. This can be seen, for example, in the reduced sleeping time during the summer compared to the winter and indicates that farm women were sacrificing their own needs during busy times, thus jeopardizing the reproduction of their own labor power over the longer term.

Increasing surplus labor time with a given necessary labor time, or reducing necessary labor time with a given surplus labor time would have increased farm women's feudal rate of exploitation, the ratio of surplus to necessary labor. In these cases, in addition to the added burden of increased exploitation, the result would have been farm wives' physical and emotional exhaustion, which increasingly found expression through the "farm woman problem."

One adjustment that was relentlessly advanced by many observers, including home extension agents, BHE researchers, and other government officials, as well as rural reformers, and periodicals like *The Farmer's Wife*, was the option of raising household labor productivity through the increased use of labor-saving home appliances and so-called modern conveniences like running water, electricity, and sinks with drains. Raising farm women's labor productivity would have allowed them to produce more in the same amount of time. If this adjustment was used to reduce the farm wife's necessary labor hours while maintaining or increasing surplus labor hours, the rate of exploitation would also have risen. The demands of making do, as discussed above, as well as women's (and the farm home's) subordinate position made achieving this solution difficult, although many women tried. Finding the necessary cash outlays proved a challenge, especially for women who lacked the ability to appropriate their own surplus. In an article entitled "600 Ways to Get That Running Water," *The Farmer's Wife* printed readers' six hundred responses to the question of how they used "psychology" to persuade their husbands to agree to that investment. Getting them carry the water themselves for a few days proved to be one of the more effective strategies, along with "calculating the net savings," "feigning illness," and "going on strike" (Kleinegger 1988, 177).

Farm families' efforts to subsidize their ancient/feudal hybrid farm enterprise participated in undermining those very subsidies by increasing the stresses and strains on farm women and their child serfs. The flight of women from rural areas is just one indicator of these tensions. Increasing numbers of women chose to leave their feudal relationships through divorce, or to remain single in the first place (Fink 1986; Fink 1992). Overwork and rural flight also contributed to farm women's reduced ability to pursue alternatives to hard work such as education, rural community-building, and even child nurturing. Rural conditions were clearly deteriorating relative to those in the cities, and children who stayed on the farm to live as their parents had done were increasingly viewed as having squandered their opportunities and their potential. As the best professionals left the countryside as well, there was growing concern that those left behind to populate the farms as well as the country churches and schools, and to provide medical care and other professional services were not likely to be the best and the brightest. Farm women's overwork played no small part in the decline. New mothers had little time to spend with their newborns after giving birth, and often lacked time to feed them properly as well. Investigators reported six-month old babies being fed things like "corn, pork, coffee, green fruit, and fried potatoes" (Danbom 1979, 8).

These problems were in addition to the ubiquitous child labor. Many young boys and girls worked as long each day as their parents did. Often their long work hours were enforced through beatings, and many young children ran away or left home as soon as they were able to escape. Reformers' enthusiasm for the intrinsic superiority of rural living and the educational qualities of rural children's work conflicted with the simultaneous concern for rural backwardness and the "arrested educational development" of children in the countryside (Gillette 1912). The shortened rural school year has already been mentioned. In addition, farm children regularly missed school when urban children did not. Rural attendance on any given day averaged 67.6 percent and urban attendance averaged 79.3 percent (Danbom 1979). Bad weather was more likely to block access to school on poorly maintained rural roads. Rural children were also more likely to miss school as a result of farm work requirements during busy times, due to poor enforcement of the compulsory education laws in rural areas. The 1923 study of children's work on Illinois farms found that almost half of the child workers reported having been absent from school for farm work during the previous year. While the most frequent duration of absence was less than 10 days, many of the children had been absent for from one to five months (Williams and Skinner 1926). The many potential obstacles for the would-be rural school child are illustrated by the story of a 10 year old boy conveyed in another Children's Bureau report. He had missed 60 percent of the school year due to field work, which did not finish until January. "Then roads and weather were so bad that his parents 'just kept him home till it was so he could go.' In February he missed seven days because 'the creek was up', and in the spring he had been ill." As a result, he had not yet completed the first grade (McGill and Merritt 1929, 30). This, combined with the fact that teachers there were apt to be young and inexperienced or incompetent, left rural people with little inclination or time for education. Few students were allowed even to finish the eighth grade, much less attend high school. This in turn contributed to the perception that lack of skill trapped those who stayed on farms.

The lack of modern conveniences or the knowledge of proper sanitary practices led to an increased incidence of hookworm, dysentery, malaria, and typhoid due to contaminated water supplies. A 1918 survey by the U.S. Public Health Service found that of 51,544 farm homes surveyed, "only 1.22 percent were equipped for the sanitary disposal of human excreta" (Danbom 1979, 8). Higher incidence of these diseases, of known cause and treatable at the time, as well as farm and household accidents due to absent mothers or children's participation in dangerous farm work, contributed to raising the rates of infant and childhood mortality in rural areas compared to cities (Fink 1986; Fink 1992).

Why did farm women continue their work of making do given these conditions? Powerful cultural processes shaping the understanding of women's work as natural, or a "labor of love," contributed to the maintenance of the work of making do. At the same time, that understanding contributed to the extraordinary burden on these women, and drew intense criticism as well. The census categorization of farm women as officially unemployed, and its impact of rendering the work of farm women largely invisible, is one formal manifestation of the social construction of farm women's work. Farm women's work was defined and (mis) understood largely in terms of passivity, or absence, and of what it was not. These qualities, in turn, were celebrated aspects of farm women themselves. Farm women were supposed to "smooth the path for others" through their work, being naturally inclined to exhibit the motherly virtues of self-sacrifice and service to family. As Florence Ward explained "motives of love and service," and the happiness of her family, were a farm wife's compensation for any hardships she might endure (Ward 1920). Making do was merely one manifestation of a woman's natural qualities.

A 1921 editorial on "Dignifying the Work of the Farm Woman" in *The Farmer's Wife* took up the criticism of the census classification, and posed the question: "Why should there be a difference in the status of work done in the home and the same work done outside the home on a commercial scale?" The difference was that women's economic contribution to the family farm went unrecognized because it was viewed as "having *saved* money instead of having *earned* it" (Neth 1998, 233). The long work hours and immense production required to generate these savings were lost in this perspective. One Kansas farm woman pointed out clearly how her family relied not only on her labor, but on the undervaluation of that labor as well:

> I protest against the hens. My husband shares the common, mistaken notion that the eggs and chickens we sell "buy the groceries." The truth is that if the fowls on our farm were charged up with all the grain they eat and the garden they destroy and half the value of the labor and care bestowed upon them they would come out in debt every time. In any fair division of labor between the farmer and his wife the man would take the outdoors and the woman the indoors. That would drop the chickens on the man's side, with the probable result that on most farms there would be no chickens.
>
> (USDA 1915, 51)

The same processes that contributed to the undervaluation of farm women's work also participated in preventing them from obtaining suitable help from others. While farm women were often required to perform nearly every kind of work in the farm household and farm enterprise as needed, evidence suggests that farm husbands rarely helped with housework, and even more rarely with childcare (Kleinegger 1988, 171; Vanek 1974). Bailey found that in only 17 percent of the Michigan families "the men carried wood and water, turned the washing machine, or did other heavier pieces of work" (Bailey 1915, 352). According to the Ward survey, recall that an average of 68 percent of farm homes lacked running water, and 61 percent of farm women reported having to carry water. This implies that in only 7 percent of cases did farm men (or someone else) regularly take responsibility for this task. It was more common for men to share occasionally in the weekly task of washing (Kleinegger 1988; Neth 1998). The 1930 USDA survey confirmed the small number of hours that men contributed to housework (two per week on average) and childcare (less than one per week on average for families with children under six), explaining that their main tasks of carrying wood, tending fires, pumping and carrying water probably took little time to complete compared to the relatively continuous tasks like preparing, serving, and cleaning up after meals, and caring for children.

The subordinate status of feudal class processes and the undervaluation of farm women's labor also meant that hired labor to help the ancient farmer had priority over hired labor to help farm women. While most farms employed hired hands throughout the year, their numbers multiplying during the summer, very few employed "hired girls" to help with the housework. Very few married women worked for wages in rural areas. Young, unmarried farmer's daughters constituted the primary available labor from which hired help (i.e. someone else's daughter), or unpaid help (i.e. one's own daughter) for farm wives was drawn. As discussed above, farm women received most of their help from their own daughters.

Bailey's study of Michigan farm homes found that 10 percent of the women surveyed had hired help for a considerable time, while 10 percent had help for a month or less during the busiest time. "Whenever help was employed, it was required by some special condition, such as illness, an unusually large family, or extra work" (Bailey and Snyder 1921, 351). The Ward survey respondents indicated that "the number of homes employing hired women the year round is almost negligible, while about 14 per cent of the 8693 families reporting employed hired women for short periods perhaps during the peak of the heavy summer work" (Ward 1920, 443).

Not only did the subordinate position of the household place limitations on the effectiveness of this solution to the farm woman problem, but so, too, did the very farm woman problem the strategy was meant to address. Both the demand for, and supply of, household serf-apprentices was constrained. The burden of overwork and lack of alternative economic opportunities in rural areas – constraints shaped by the serfdom of farm women – contributed to the outmigration of farm daughters from rural areas (which, in turn, compounded the problem of overwork for the women who remained). In his report on the 1915 Houston survey, Mitchell noted that the disparity between rural and urban living standards affected the farm woman "chiefly by drawing away those from whom she might otherwise obtain assistance" and went on to recommend the establishment of "official employment bureaus" to "divert the stream of immigrants from the cities to the country" (Mitchell 1915). A 1915 rural sociology textbook noted the problem of female outmigration thus: "Sometimes the drudgery of the farm is endured by the mother uncomplainingly, or even contentedly; but the daughter recoils from it with a growing discontent" (Kleinegger 1988). One Iowa farm woman portrayed this tension between mothers and daughters. "Neither one of them was ever farmers when they was on the farm" (Neth 1998, 569). She continued, explaining her own complicity in aiding her daughters' rebellion. "I was quite a farmer. More of a farmer than my husband.... I had to milk cows and do those kind of things, but I never expected my girls to do it and they never did"

(Neth 1998, 569). Like her, many farm women may have been reluctant to train their daughters for future rural serfdom, encouraging them instead to seek their living elsewhere (Neth 1998, 569).

Conclusion

Family farm life was hard for everyone involved. Men, women, and children worked long hours doing strenuous work for minimal and uncertain compensation in relative isolation, with little time for many diversions including education, and few alternative economic opportunities. The ancient/feudal hybrid class structure was a stable class structural form, yet the very strategies undertaken for its survival threw it constantly into a potential state of crisis. Persistence rates of less than 50 percent in some areas during this period meant that many family farms simply were not able to cope with these contradictions (Fink 1992). Class crisis did not signal class transition, however. While individual farmers and their families may have fallen on hard times and been forced to sell out, the ancient-feudal hybrid continued as the dominant class structural form among family farms that remained.

As discussed above, powerful countervailing forces were at work to hold those that remained to bear the burden of their respective class responsibilities. That burden weighed heavily on the shoulders of farm women and children as they bore the additional injustice of exploitation in their roles as feudal serfs. No wonder that journalist Herbert Quick wrote in 1913, "I have found the men on farms much more contented and happy than the women" (Fink 1992, 156).

The farm woman problem emerged in part from the peculiar relation among the class structures constituting the family farm hybrid and from its contradictory conditions of existence. The farm woman problem in turn provoked further changes in those class structures. The Country Life movement brought attention to the farm woman problem in particular and to the problems of rural life in general, in part because of the glaring discrepancy between the glossy agrarian ideal and the gritty reality for most farm families. In shining the spotlight on family farms, reformers and observers increased farm women's own awareness of their situation, and empowered them to speak and learn about it, and to propose solutions. Reformers and government agents brought their own solutions as well. While many, especially farm women themselves, expressed the need for some kind of radical restructuring of their lives, the main thrust of these efforts, stemming from the Country Life movement, was to make farm families more receptive to the adoption of new labor-saving technologies in farm and home production, and to the application of the principles of scientific management to their labor processes.

Reformers and farm women alike lacked the language or even awareness of class that would have led them to address the exploitative class structures contributing to their situation. And so they ultimately failed to resolve the farm woman problem. Hence, new labor-saving technologies in ancient farm production progressively lightened the load of farm men's work, but the discrepancy between the conditions of farmer and wife continued, as making life easier for the farmer often translated into an added burden of "making do" for his wife. Similarly, time use studies from the 1940s, 50s, and 60s showed that both rural and urban women's household work time remained remarkably consistent (Cowan 1985; Vanek 1974). Hence, even when they did gain access to labor-saving technologies in the home, women were not able to "save" their own labor, but continued to subsidize that of others, increasing the relative surplus they delivered to their feudal appropriators. Long before urban women began to experience the second shift of paid labor alongside their household work, farm women worked a double shift in farm and household production. When their labor on the farm was no longer enough, farm women went out to find jobs in the paid labor force. Today, researchers confirm that many farm women continue to work a double, or even a triple shift of work – and, even when they are the primary breadwinners for the family, they still describe that work and the income they earn as "helping out" (Gallagher and Delworth 1993; Naples 1994). The farm woman problem was never resolved, in part, because it was a "feudal" woman problem, exacerbated by farm women's obligation to subsidize their husband's "independence."

Susan Glaspell's 1917 short story, "A Jury of Her Peers", is instructive. It tells the story of a farmer/husband found murdered in his isolated house (Glaspell 1918). The sheriff and some men, accompanied by their wives, go to investigate the murder and to collect some things for the farmer's wife. While the men search around for clues to the perpetrator's identity they leave their wives in the kitchen. As the women look around, they realize that the so-called "insignificant kitchen things" hold the key to solving the farmhouse murder. The many jars of preserves on the shelves, put up in the hot weather, the shabby, "well-worn" clothing, the old stove, the water pail on the counter, and other things indicate the farm wife's dreary, lonely, and needlessly inhumane existence. As realization dawns, one of the ladies exclaims,

> We live close together, and we live far apart. We all go through the same things—it's all just a different kind of the same thing! If it weren't—why do you and I *understand?* Why do we *know*—what we know this minute?

These women, like many others, were aware that they suffered injustice due to their shared experiences as farm women and feudal serfs. Yet they were also unable to name the "invisible violence" stemming from their exploitation. The ladies in the story continued by covering up the crime, apparently in silent acquiescence that this, at least, had been a justifiable act of violence.

Notes

1 According to the Census Bureau definition, the Midwest includes Ohio, Indiana, Illinois, Michigan, Wisconsin, Minnesota, Iowa, Nebraska, North Dakota, South Dakota, Kansas, and Missouri. This corresponds roughly with the area included in the Corn Belt, defined as the portion of the Midwest where corn has traditionally been the dominant crop. The Corn Belt includes the primary corn-producing states of Iowa, Indiana, Illinois, and Ohio, as well as portions of neighboring states.

2   According to Fink (1992), the rural sociologist George Beal dates the possible first use of the term as 1914.

3   In equation form, the family farm's feudal class structure can be mapped as follows:

$$\textit{Feudal Class Structure: } SL(F)^{FFH} + SL(F)^{FFE} = SSCP(F)^{FFH} + SSCP(F)^{FFE}$$

The terms $SL(F)^{FFH}$ and $SL(F)^{FFE}$ stand, respectively, for the feudal surplus labor $(SL(F))$ of farm women in the family farm household (superscript FFH) and in the family farm enterprise (superscript FFE). Likewise, the two terms on the right hand side stand for subsumed class payments ($SSCP$) to secure conditions of existence for the feudal class process in both the family farm household (superscript FFH) and the family farm enterprise (superscript FFE).

4   In equation form, the family farm's ancient class structure can be mapped as follows:

$$\textit{Ancient Class Structure: } SL(A)^{FFE} = SSCP(A)^{FFE}$$

The terms $SL(A)^{FFE}$ and $SSCP(A)^{FFE}$ stand respectively for the ancient surplus labor of farm men in the family farm enterprise, and the requisite subsumed class payments to secure the conditions of existence for this class process.

5   The Census Bureau classified farm women along with other housewives as officially unemployed.

6   BHE researchers appear to have classified the time for eating meals as non-working time for personal care, while others classified this time as working time. For example, Bailey specifically noted that mealtimes were worktimes since farm wives were still "on duty" and expected to serve others, even while they were eating. This difference in classification would amount to an average of 1 hour's difference in reported worktime per day (Bailey 1915; Bailey and Snyder 1921; Kneeland 1932).

7   Researchers found little variation in the workday across geographical regions, so I have included in the discussion surveys of farm women outside the Midwestern region. Indeed, the lack of variation in the workday is in itself a remarkable fact, as discussed further below (Vanek 1974; Vanek 1980).

8   If farm men and their employees or family apprentice-helpers performed the work, the poultry and dairy were considered to be primarily ancient farm commodities and took precedence over other products (and those who labored to produce them) whether these were marketed or not. This may explain why relatively fewer women were responsible for milking as opposed to gathering eggs, for example, since dairy products were more likely to be produced and marketed by male farmers as ancient farm commodities (USDA 1915, 17).

9   This "agricultural exceptionalism" survives today in the Fair Labor Standards Act (FLSA), which established federal minimum wage, overtime, and youth employment standards for most workers in 1938. Exceptions included agricultural workers. While non-family wage workers in agriculture have succeeded in winning some of these protections, there are still no minimum wage, overtime, or age restrictions for youth employed on their parents' farms (U.S. Department of Labor 2008; U.S. Department of Labor 2011).

10   Children working on home farms also included the thousands of orphaned or neglected children who were "indentured" to local farm families by various "child-saving" institutions throughout the Midwest, such as the Wisconsin State Public School and the Nebraska Child Saving Institute (Riney-Kehrberg 2005).

11   As Pamela Riney-Kehrberg argues, this belief in the virtue of agricultural work and agricultural families was reflected in the "child-saving" institutions throughout the Midwest, as well as the "orphan trains" from the New York Children's Aid Society. Through these institutions, hundreds of children were shipped away from cities and indentured to farm families, even as others were choosing to leave the countryside for the cities in greater numbers (Riney-Kehrberg 2005).

12 The following equations express the interdependence between the feudal and ancient class structures in terms of the transfer of appropriated surplus between them:

Feudal Class Structure: $SL(F) - Y_i + NCR_j < SSCP(F)$
Ancient Farmer's Consumption: $NL(A) + NCR_i - Y_j = \hat{C}(A) + \hat{C}_F$

The term $SL(F)$ is feudal surplus labor in the family farm household and family farm enterprise; $SSCP(F)$ are feudal subsumed class payments for the reproduction of feudal class processes in the family farm household and family farm enterprise. Y_i and NCR_i stand for the feudal subsidy flowing from the feudal class structure to subsidize the ancient farmer's personal consumption; likewise Y_j and NCR_j stand for the ancient subsidy and its corresponding non-class revenue flow to the feudal class structure. $NL(A)$ is ancient necessary labor, and the terms on the right hand side of the second equation stand for the goods and services made available for the ancient farmer's consumption, either from the wage he pays himself, $\hat{C}(A)$, or from the portion of his wife's feudal surplus labor diverted to his consumption, $\hat{C}_F$.

13 The following equation illustrates this circumstance:

Ancient Class Structure: $SL(A)^{FFE} > SSCP(A)^{FFE}$

$SL(A)^{FFE}$ is the ancient surplus labor in the family farm enterprise and $SSCP(A)^{FFE}$ is ancient subsumed class payments for the family farm enterprise.

14 The following equation reproduces the terms from the feudal class structural equation in note 12, with the addition of arrows which represent the discussion of making do and its impact on the reproduction of the family farm's feudal class structure:

Feudal Class Structure: $\uparrow SL(F) - \uparrow Y_i + \downarrow NCR_j = \downarrow SSCP(F)$

As shown, the budget for the feudal class structure is balanced by the farm wife's strategy of making do, as well as the addition of the feudal surplus labor of her children.

15 A 1953 study showed that on more prosperous farms, there was a greater distance between the barn and the house (Kleinegger 170).

16 This is opposed to feudal farm commodities, like eggs, produced by farm women. Egg production was a form of farm production, hence occurred in the family farm enterprise. However, farm women usually took care of poultry alone, hence the commodities they produced were feudal, even though their labor occurred in the hybrid family farm enterprise, in which both ancient and feudal class processes regularly but separately occurred.

17 The following equation expresses the helping out strategy in class terms:

Ancient/Feudal Hybrid Class Structure: $\left[SL(A) + SL(F)\right]_{HY}^{FFE} > SSCP(A)^{FFE}$

The bracketed terms on the left hand side depict the surplus labor produced in hybrid farm production in the family farm enterprise (indicated by the superscript "FFE" and the subscript "HY"). Child serfs and farmer serf-apprentices performed feudal surplus labor ($SL(F)$) alongside the ancient farmer ($SL(A)$). The brackets indicate that the commodity produced was a hybrid commodity because the labor processes occurred along with the ancient and feudal class processes at the same time. The term on the right hand side depicts the ancient subsumed class payments.

18 Other factors may have included lack of transportation or poor rural transportation or communication infrastructure. Studies showed that even when farm families owned a car or even a telephone, many women lacked the authority to decide their use, claim their use, or operate them (Jellison 1993).

19 The following equation expresses the farm wife's day in class terms:

$NL(F) + SL(F) + X(F, A) + R = 24$

The terms on the left hand side stand, respectively for feudal necessary and surplus labor time, feudal and ancient subsumed class labor time, and residual time.

82   *The family farm hybrid*

References

Bailey, Ilena M. 1915. "A Study of the Management of the Farm Home." *The Journal of Home Economics* 7 (1): 348–353.
Bailey, Ilena M., and Snyder, Melissa F. 1921. "A Survey of Farm Homes." *The Journal of Home Economics* 13 (8): 346–356.
Bruère, Martha Bensley, and Robert Walter Bruère. 1912. "Revolt of the Farmer's Wife." *Harper's Bazaar*, March.
Carter, Susan B., Scott Sigmund Gartner, Michael R. Haines, Alan L. Olmstead, Richard Sutch, and Gavin Wright, eds. 2006. *Historical Statistics of the United States, Earliest Times to the Present: Millennial Edition Online*. New York: Cambridge University Press. Available online at http://hsus.cambridge.org/HSUSWeb/HSUSEntryServlet.
Casey, Janet Galligani. 2004. " 'This Is Your Magazine': Domesticity, Agrarianism, and *The Farmer's Wife*." *American Periodicals: A Journal of History, Criticism, and Bibliography* 14 (2): 179–211.
Clark, Marjorie Ruth, and Greta Gray. 1930. "The Routine and Seasonal Work of Nebraska Farm Women." *Bulletin University of Nebraska College of Agriculture* 238: 5–39.
Country Life Commission. 1917. "Report of the Commission on Country Life." New York: Sturgis & Walton.
Cowan, Ruth Schwartz. 1985. *More Work For Mother: The Ironies Of Household Technology From The Open Hearth To The Microwave*. New York: Basic Books.
Danbom, David B. 1979. *The Resisted Revolution: Urban America and the Industrialization of Agriculture, 1900–1930*. Ames: Iowa State University Press.
Duby, Georges. 1968. *Rural Economy and Country Life in the Medieval West*. Translated by Cynthia Postan. London: Edward Arnold.
E. G. R., Mrs. 1924. "Have an Allowance." *The Farmer's Wife*, November.
Fink, Deborah. 1986. *Open Country, Iowa: Rural Women, Tradition and Change*. Albany: State University of New York Press.
Fink, Deborah. 1992. *Agrarian Women: Wives and Mothers in Rural Nebraska, 1880–1940*. Studies in Rural Culture. Chapel Hill and London: University of North Carolina Press.
Fraad, Harriet, Stephen Resnick, and Richard Wolff. 1994. *Bringing It All Back Home*. London and Boulder, CO: Pluto Press.
Friedberger, Mark. 1983. "The Farm Family and the Inheritance Process: Evidence from the Corn Belt, 1870–1950." *Agricultural History* 57 (1) (January 1): 1–13.
Gabriel, Satyananda. 1989. "Ancients: a Marxian Theory of Self-exploitation." PhD Dissertation. Amherst, MA: University of Massachusetts.
Gallagher, Elizabeth, and Ursula Delworth. 1993. "The Third Shift: Juggling Employment, Family, and the Farm." *Journal of Rural Community Psychology* 12: 21–36.
Galpin, Charles Josiah. 1918. *Rural Life*. New York: The Century Company.
Gardner, Bruce L. 2006. *American Agriculture in the Twentieth Century: How It Flourished and What It Cost*. Cambridge: Harvard University Press.
Garkovich, Lorraine, and Janet Bokemeier. 1988. "Agricultural Mechanization and American Farm Women's Economic Roles." In *Women and Farming*, edited by Wava Haney and Jane Knowles, 211–228. Rural Studies. Boulder and London: Westview Press.
Gillette, John M. 1912. "Rural Child Labor." Child Labor Bulletin Volume 1. National Child Labor Committee. June.

Glaspell, Susan. 1918. *"A Jury of Her Peers" The Best Short Stories of 1917*. Boston: Small, Maynard, & Co.

Hurt, Douglas R. 2003. *Problems of Plenty: The American Farmer in the Twentieth Century*. Chicago: Ivan R Dee.

Jefferson, Thomas. 1853. *Notes on the State of Virginia*. Richmond, VA: J. W. Randolph.

Jellison, Katherine. 1993. *Entitled to Power*. Chapel Hill: University of North Carolina Press.

Kirkpatrick, Ellis Lore. 1929. *The Farmer's Standard of Living*. New York: The Century Company.

Kleinegger, Christine. 1988. "Out of the Barns and into the Kitchens: Transformations in Farm Women's Work in the First Half of the Twentieth Century." In *Women, Work, and Technology: Transformations*, edited by Barbara Drygulski Wright. Women and Culture. Ann Arbor: University of Michigan Press.

Kline, Ronald R. 1997. "Ideology and Social Surveys: Reinterpreting the Effects of 'Laborsaving' Technology on American Farm Women." *Technology and Culture* 38 (2) (April 1): 355–385.

Kneeland, Hildegarde. 1928. "Women on Farms Average 63 Hours' Work Weekly in Survey of 700 Homes." In *Yearbook of Agriculture 1928*, 620–622. Washington, DC: Government Printing Office.

Kneeland, Hildegarde. 1932. "Leisure of Home Makers Studied for Light on Standards of Living." In *Yearbook of Agriculture 1932*, 562–564. Washington, DC: Government Printing Office.

Knowles, Jane. 1988. "'It's Our Turn Now': Rural American Women Speak Out, 1900–1920." In *Women and Farming*, edited by Wava Haney and Jane Knowles, 303–318. Rural Studies. London and Boulder: Westview Press.

L. R. H., Mrs. 1914. "Little Fellow Helps." *The Farmer's Wife*, April.

Lauters, Amy Mattson. 2009. *More Than a Farmer's Wife: Voices of American Farm Women, 1910–1960*. Columbia: University of Missouri Press.

Lovett, Laura L. 2007. *Conceiving the Future: Pronatalism, Reproduction, and the Family in the United States, 1890–1938*. Chapel Hill: University of North Carolina Press.

Macy, Loring K. 1938. *Changes in Technology and Labor Requirements in Crop Production: Corn*. Works Progress Administration. Washington, DC: Government Printing Office.

Martini, Dinah Duffy. 2003. "Technological Change in US Agriculture: The Case of Substitution of Gasoline Tractor Power for Horse Power." PhD Dissertation. University of Washington.

McGill, Nettie Pauline, and Ella Arvilla Merritt. 1929. "Children in Agriculture." Department of Labor, Children's Bureau 114. Washington, DC: Government Printing Office. Available online at http://archive.org/details/childreninagricu00mcgi.

Mitchell, Edward B. 1915. "The American Farm Woman as She Sees Herself." In *Yearbook of Agriculture*. Washington, DC: Government Printing Office.

Moore, Elizabeth. 1917. "Maternity and Infant Care in a Rural County in Kansas." Department of Labor, Children's Bureau 26. Rural Child Welfare Series. Washington, DC: Government Printing Office.

Moore, Ruth. 1930. "Farm Home Makers Get Little Aid in Housework from Others in Family." In *Yearbook of Agriculture 1928*, 241–243. Washington, DC: Government Printing Office.

Moorehouse, L.A. 1921. "Labor and Material Requirements of Field Crops." United

States Department of Agriculture Bulletin No. 1000. Washington, DC: Government Printing Office.

Naples, Nancy. 1994. "Contradictions in Agrarian Ideology: Restructuring Gender, Race-Ethnicity, and Class." *Rural Sociology* 59 (1): 110–135.

Neth, Mary C. 1998. *Preserving the Family Farm: Women, Community, and the Foundations of Agribusiness in the Midwest, 1900–1940.* Baltimore: The Johns Hopkins University Press.

Patri, Angelo. 1926. "The Child's Work." *The Farmer's Wife*, October.

Rankin, J. 1928. "The Use of Time in Farm Homes." Agricultural Experiment Station Bulletin. Lincoln: University of Nebraska College of Agriculture Experiment Station.

Resnick, Stephen A., and Richard D. Wolff. 2009. "The Class Analysis of Households Extended: Children, Fathers, and Family Budgets." In *Class Struggle on the Home Front Work, Conflict, and Exploitation in the Household*, edited by Graham Cassano, 86–115. London and New York: Palgrave Macmillan.

Riney-Kehrberg, Pamela. 2005. *Childhood on the Farm: Work, Play, and Coming of Age in the Midwest.* Lawrence: University Press of Kansas.

Sachs, Carolyn E. 1983. *The Invisible Farmers: Women in Agricultural Production.* Totowa, NJ: Rowman & Allanheld.

Sherbon, Florence Brown, and Elizabeth Moore. 1919. "Maternity and Infant Care in Two Rural Counties in Wisconsin." Department of Labor, Children's Bureau 4. Rural Child Welfare Series. Washington, DC: U.S. Government Printing Office.

The Farmer's Wife. 1928. "A Portrait: The Typical Farm Homemaker." 9 (July): 33.

The Farmer's Wife. 1920. "The Stability of the Country." (May).

The Ladies' Home Journal. 1909. "Is This the Trouble With the Farmer's Wife?" February.

The Literary Digest. 1919. "Some Solid Reasons for a Strike of Farm Wives." December 20.

The New York Times. 1915. "Farm Women Find Life Hard." May 30.

Tuttle, G. W. 1919. "Mischievous Idle Hands." *The Farmer's Wife*, January.

United States Department of Agriculture (USDA). 1915. "Social and Labor Needs of Farm Women." 103. Washington, DC: Government Printing Office.

U.S. Department of Labor. 2008. "Fact Sheet #12: Agricultural Employers Under the Fair Labor Standards Act (FLSA)." U.S. Wage and Hour Division. July.

U.S. Department of Labor. 2011. "Handy Reference Guide to the Fair Labor Standards Act." U.S. Wage and Hour Division. April.

Vanek, Joann. 1974. "Time Spent in Housework." *Scientific American* 231 (November): 116–120.

Vanek, Joann. 1980. "Work, and Family Work, Leisure, and Family Roles: Farm Households in the United States, 1920–1955." *Journal of Family History* 5 (December 1): 422–431.

Ward, Florence. 1920. "The Farm Woman's Problems." *The Journal of Home Economics* 12 (10) (October): 437–457.

Williams, Dorothy, and Mary E. Skinner. 1926. "Work of Children on Illinois Farms." Department of Labor, Children's Bureau 168. Washington, DC: Government Printing Office.

3 Technical change, ancient competition, and the hunt for super profits

Chapter 2 focused on the transfers of value between the different kinds of class structures within the same family farm, showing how the survival of the family farm has been predicated on a ruthless exploitation of farm women and children in rural life. Now, Chapter 3 adds to the analysis by examining the transfers of value between ancient class structures in family farm enterprises and non-farm enterprises or government. It examines the patterns of market interaction and competition among farmers shaping and shaped by these value transfers called super profits, and between farmers and non-farm agribusiness and government. Specifically, I apply and extend the model of competition and the hunt for super profit developed by Resnick (2006). I show how the survival of the family farm has been connected to a ruthless competition in which some farmers cannibalize others and non-farm agribusinesses thrive on the carnage, as well as to state policies which actually serve to intensify this perpetual crisis that mainly benefits the few at the expense of the many.

U.S. agriculture crossed a watershed of development sometime during the interwar period so that, by the start of World War II, the outlines of a new system were discernible. The object of this chapter is to explain the origins of that system using a Marxian class analysis of the scramble for super profits among ancient corn farmers during the 1920s and 1930s. Agriculture shifted from an expanding to a contracting industry by many measures, and the accompanying decline signaled severe economic distress and rural dislocation. The 1920s and 1930s were periods of particularly sustained crisis. Farm employment began declining, as did the number of farms and farmers. With relatively stable land in farms, the average size of farms began increasing, while millions of small farmers nevertheless persisted. Farmers and their families began migrating in larger numbers to cities, leaving shrinking rural communities increasingly bereft of economic opportunity. Yet, while millions of family farms began suffering ongoing crisis and failure, they achieved extraordinary success in terms of productivity growth, an agricultural revolution of unprecedented magnitude. This was also the beginning of unprecedented government intervention in the agricultural economy.

After having nearly ground to a halt between 1900 and 1920, productivity and output resumed their ascension, particularly after 1935. The average annual growth rate in total factor productivity from 1948 to 2009 in agriculture (1.52 percent) exceeded that in the non-farm economy (approximately 1.2 percent) (Ball et al. 2012). Figure 3.1 documents this achievement in the case of corn production. Labor hours per one hundred bushels drifted downward until the Great Depression, then rose slightly before beginning a steep decline just as farm programs were enacted. During the long, post-World War II economic expansion, then, no other sector outperformed agriculture in terms of productivity growth. In severe decline, subject to massive government intervention, family farms became the most technologically dynamic enterprises in the United States.

This chapter is organized as follows: I begin this introductory section by presenting the historical background – explaining the rise of industrial agriculture, and the transition from the "farm woman problem" to the "farm problem." I then turn to discussing the processes and ramifications of one of the technical changes, the adoption of the farm tractor, which began on Midwestern family farms in the 1920s, to set the stage for the take-off in productivity growth along with the dramatic changes which accompanied that accomplishment. After first presenting an overview of the case of the farm tractor, I then explain how that technical change was shaped by competition among family farms in a hunt for super profits, or what agricultural historian Willard Cochrane refers to as the "technology treadmill" (1993). In the third section of the chapter, I explain how these developments were further shaped and supported by state policy beginning in the 1930s, reinforcing the technical trends as set forth in the Country Life agenda and advanced by the USDA, some farmers, agribusiness and related commercial concerns including farm creditors. These competitive processes and

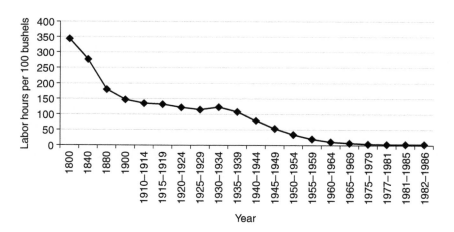

Figure 3.1 Labor hours per 100 bushels of corn, 1800–1986 (data from Carter, Susan B., Scott Sigmund Gartner, Michael R. Haines, Alan L. Olmstead, Richard Sutch, and Gavin Wright, eds. 2006. *Historical Statistics of the United States, Earliest Times to the Present: Millennial Edition Online*. New York: Cambridge University Press. Available online at http://hsus.cambridge.org/HSUSWeb/HSUSEntryServlet).

state policies rewarded larger, landowning ancient farmers who borrowed to finance their purchases of new land and equipment. I examine how the competitive hunt for super profits was mediated by state policy, and is then linked to prominent features of subsequent agricultural development, including rapid technical change and the industrialization of farm production, the rise of agribusiness, chronic crisis and radical restructuring among farmers, and the entrenchment of farm programs. Finally, in the concluding section, I examine the ramifications of technical changes and state policies for family farm class structures and survival strategies. While most accounts of these structural shifts begin after World War II, the take-off in productivity growth actually occurred during the Great Depression (Clarke 2002). I focus on the interwar period and argue that the post-war changes are more properly understood as rooted in this important transitional period and linked to the farm woman problem.

Industrial agriculture

All of these developments are associated with the arrival of "industrial agriculture" and an accompanying technological "revolution" in U.S. farming. Twentieth-century technical change in agricultural production occurred along three related fronts: mechanical, biological, and chemical. Together, these constituted a new system in which an industrial model of production was increasingly applied to methods of farming. Industrialization in agriculture began with the mechanization of the wheat farms in the Dakotas, California, and the Great Plains after 1900, and soon spread to other crops, including corn (Clarke 2002). Industrialization was accompanied by transformations in the act of farming, as well as in the broader agricultural system.

The adoption of these new mechanical, chemical, and biological technologies meant that farmers increasingly purchased inputs which substituted for those previously produced on the farm. The internal combustion engine (tractors and trucks), began rapidly replacing animal power (horses and mules) in the 1920s in all aspects of the production of crops, from soil preparation and cultivation, to planting, harvesting, and hauling finished products. This required the increasing use of commercial fertilizers to replace animal fertilizer, previously produced by horses and mules. These, along with other chemicals to control weeds and insects, increasingly came onto farms in the 1920s and 1930s, although rapid adoption did not occur until during and after World War II.[1] Lastly, purchased hybrid corn seeds replaced non-hybrid, open-pollinated varieties in an extremely rapid process of adoption beginning in the 1930s. One of the leading historians of industrialization in U.S. agriculture, Deborah Fitzgerald, explains, "Discrete activities were thereby transformed into industrial practices and reintroduced onto farms as inputs" (Fitzgerald 2003, 3). By the late 1960s, the basic elements of today's industrial agriculture model had been widely adopted. In 1959, *Time* magazine hailed the new "pushbutton cornucopia," observing optimistically that the same "assembly line techniques" applied in industry could be applied in agriculture as well (*Time* March 9).

Not only did various production processes move off the farm and into industrial factories, but farms came to look and act more like factories in many ways as well. As the metaphor implies, innovations were linked with a shift toward an "industrial logic" in farming. The "New Agriculture" involved the modernization of farming through the application of methods of factory production and scientific management, such as those exemplified by Henry Ford.

Farmers adopted new ideas, practices, and relationships with a complex web of interdependence accompanying each new innovation. Farmers were increasingly located in what conservationist Benton MacKaye called in 1925 an "industrial web" and a "physiology of industrial empire" (in Fitzgerald 2003, 3). Economist William N. Parket called it "vertical disintegration," as farms spun off functions and became "small factories pouring industrial inputs into the land over the year and extracting a raw product for immediate sale" (Clarke 2002, 9). Lighthall and Roberts call this process "capitalist integration," or the "expansion in the total share of surplus in production for agribusiness corporations via a progressively greater dependence of farmers on advanced production technologies" (Lighthall and Roberts 1995, 323).

As with industry, these changes had far-reaching impacts on farmers and their families. Farmers traded reduced risk for reduced flexibility and role in the management of their production processes. Once they switched, they found the increased cash expenses difficult to manage. Nevertheless, farmers who climbed on the "technology treadmill," found they could not afford to get off unless they quit farming altogether. The interwar period marked the beginning of the massive outmigration from rural areas and the increasing role of agribusiness in the farm economy as the adoption of the factory farming model led to the rise of large-scale, specialized farms, mass producing standardized products rapidly and with less need for skilled labor (or labor of any kind).

From the "farm woman problem" to the "farm problem"

The end of World War I corresponded with the close of the long period of farm prosperity which reached its peak with a sharp wartime spike in farm prices from 1914 to 1920. This ushered in a longer period of chronic decline punctuated by occasional acute crises, a situation that would persist for the remainder of the twentieth century. In the two year period from 1919 to 1921, net farm income declined from a peak of $9 billion to just $3.4 billion, the lowest point of the century until then (Carter et al. 2006; Gardner 2006).[2] An eight year "age of uncertainty" for farmers precipitated by the post-war sag in European demand "ended" only with the certainty of the onset of the Great Depression in 1929, as the rest of the country finally followed farmers into the economic doldrums. These developments marked both short term crises, as well as longer term structural shifts, characterizing a new phase of rapid technical change, chronic overproduction, falling prices, rising costs, and waves of farm bankruptcies. Both the wartime prosperity and the farm depression that followed set the stage for these changes, and the shift from "the farm woman problem" to the now more familiar "farm problem."

In 1940, the USDA issued a report that placed the blame for the farm problem on the "maladjustment" precipitated by the sharp increase in demand for U.S. farm products accompanying World War I. While the USDA report implied that these maladjustments were temporary, many of the problems identified in the report persisted, and similar episodes of crisis have replayed again and again. In this particular episode, farmers seeking to take advantage of the wartime windfall responded exuberantly to patriotic appeals to "Plow to the Fence for National Defense!" finding 40 million extra acres to plow under for food production during this period (USDA 1940a, 3). Farm prices remained high, in spite of efforts to increase production to meet the demand, provoking a rapid increase in land prices fueled further by speculation. Land prices peaked in 1920 at a level that was 70 percent higher than the 1912–14 average. Many farmers borrowed heavily on the basis of wartime prices to finance purchases of new land and equipment to expand production. Average mortgage debt per acre in 1920 was 135 percent above that of 1910 (USDA 1940a, 5).

Prices tumbled following World War I as European producers geared up to achieve food self-sufficiency, while other supplying nations, newly-arrived on the world market, also found themselves without their European markets and became new sources of competition for U.S. farmers. Land prices quickly followed farm prices, and many farmers found themselves unable to meet their loan obligations. Farm bankruptcies spiked as farmers' purchasing power declined along with their share of national income. The USDA summed up the situation thus: "Farmers had more acres producing more efficiently for market, with smaller market outlets, a greatly increased debt burden, and drastically reduced prices for their products" (USDA 1940a, 5). While prices recovered somewhat following the initial shock, the situation for many farmers remained grim throughout the decade of the 1920s.

As a result of the farm depression, attention to the "farm woman problem" began to fade, and shifted instead to the "farm problem." Since the former was never really resolved, however, its continued existence shaped the context for the resolution of the latter. The second prong of the two-pronged Country Life agenda, that of rural uplift and social change, was discarded in favor of a singular and narrowed focus on promoting the "New Agriculture" or the improvement of farm business practices, mechanization, and the development of scientific farming methods. The shift was a reflection of the shift in general political sentiment away from Progressivism with its emphasis on social criticism and broad social change, and toward conservativism, as represented in Warren G. Harding's 1921 inaugural plea for "not revolution, but restoration." In agriculture, the shift toward conservativism was reflected in the growing influence of the American Farm Bureau Federation, or Farm Bureau, a private agricultural institution composed mainly of wealthy owners of large farms. Formed in 1920, the organization was a coalition of state farm bureaus with a nationwide membership of 320,000 in 28 states. The Farm Bureau served the interests of big farm businesses – large, commercial, land-owning farmers – and worked closely with government extension services to help farmers pursue competitiveness through increased productivity (Hurt 2003). Harding's secretary of agriculture, Henry C. Wallace, was a supporter of the group, which exercised considerable influence on government farm policy throughout the 1920s.

Even though (and probably also because) many farm women had seen little improvement in their situation, they no longer found the same outlets available to voice their protests. The broader push for equal status in the farm home lost considerable momentum when women won the right to vote in 1920. Having never really identified the role of class exploitation in their situation, and without this unifying issue, farm women lost the full political force of the feminist movement in their criticism of the inequities of farm life. The tone of the popular press changed, with articles and letters expressing offense and disagreement with the representations of farm women as overworked and deprived, and those extolling the virtues and satisfaction of rural life appearing prominently (Kline 1997, 365). The USDA also shifted to a more optimistic portrayal of farm women's situations. A 1923 report on a survey of farm women and farm women's letters to *The Farmer's Wife* found many of the same issues expressed by women in Houston's 1915 survey, yet the report focused on the "happy and forward-looking farm women" for whom the joys of farm life outweighed any problems (Kline 1997, 365; Jellison 1993, 27). The formation of the Bureau of Home Economics in 1923 symbolized this new shift in official policy toward farm women. Its focus was on helping them to become better homemakers, creating a domestic haven for their farm businessmen husbands just as urban women were supposed to do for their non-farm businessmen husbands. Labor-saving farm equipment would help facilitate farm women's domesticity. Broader issues of rural women's health, education, social life, and economic status were no longer on the USDA agenda (Jellison 1993, 26–32).

One reason for this shift was that the continuing farm depression meant that the official recommended "solution" of labor-saving equipment for the farm home remained beyond the reach of many farm families (even as labor-saving equipment for the farm continued to be a focus of reform efforts). The causation also went the other way. That is, the inability to afford labor-saving equipment for the home contributed to the lack of resolution to the farm woman problem and hence the continued undervaluation of farm women's labor. On the other hand, and just as importantly, the lack of resolution to the farm woman problem, and hence the continued undervaluation of farm women's labor, helped shape the perception that farm families could not "afford" labor-saving equipment for the farm home, even as that same undervalued labor made the purchase of farm equipment possible.

Also gone was any reference to the solution of production cooperatives such as laundries and creameries which many farm women had suggested and which had met with considerable success in some communities (USDA 1915). While the USDA was at first supportive of these measures, and marketing cooperatives still remain common for farm enterprises today, farm and home production cooperatives were quickly passed over in official policy in favor of a focus on individual solutions through purchases of new equipment. Thus, official policy contributed to maintaining family farm isolation, while encouraging farmers' dependence on capitalist industry supplying farm and home implements as well as other inputs.

The slump also meant that focus shifted away from inequalities within the family farm, and toward inequalities between the farm and non-farm sectors. Agricultural goals, for example, were formulated in terms of various measures of parity, or the balance of purchasing power between farmers and non-farmers, to assess the degree of "imbalance" that had developed between the two sectors since the Golden Age when the ratio of incomes and prices was deemed to be "fair" and "balanced" (although, even then, the quality of rural living was still widely acknowledged to be inferior to that of urban life) (USDA 1940a, 19; Casey 2004). Much as farm women's work was viewed as secondary to that of their farmer husband, the "farm woman problem" became subsumed within the "farm problem."

The rosy rhetoric notwithstanding, the intractability of the farm woman problem (and of overworked farm family members in general) constrained possible strategies for resolving the farm problem. The choice of technical change, with all of its accompanying problems cannot be fully understood without this context, which I presented in the previous chapter. As discussed there, the use of family labor was one way that family farms remained viable, yet the contradictory result, of which the farm woman problem was one manifestation, was that the use of undervalued family labor was stretched to its limit. Hired labor was scarce and expensive, and likely to be even more so during crucial periods when crops were most vulnerable. Each stage of crop production – planting, cultivating, picking, and hauling – had to be completed in a timely manner or else risk damage to the crop. In any case, the presence of hired hands often increased the burden of work on farm women. Thus there was limited opportunity to increase production and absolute surplus by working the family and hired laborers for longer hours. Not much more labor could be squeezed from women, children, or farmers themselves. The successes of feudalism presented a limit to further ancient expansion. Internal feudal to ancient subsidies needed to be supplemented in some way.

The solution that had worked until the closing of the frontier around 1910, was to rely on ever-expanding acres of land under cultivation (and hence increasing the rural population as well) as the frontier moved westward. After 1910, there was increased emphasis on more intensively working existing acreage by improving the efficiency and scientific management of farm production practices. The limits of both ancient and feudal exploitation combined to provide conditions of existence for the introduction of labor saving machines and technologies into ancient farm production as a viable long term strategy for weathering crises or for expanding during prosperous times. Thus, the farm woman problem served to reinforce the new focus of government policies, and conservative farm and business interests, pushing the technology strategy for family farms. Hence, while technical change, mechanization, and "scientific" farming were partly to blame for the post-war farm slump as these had helped create the hangover of oversupply, they also remained features of family farming in the Corn Belt, the "solution" to the problems of the agricultural imbalances they had helped to create and thereby perpetuate.

In the next section of the chapter, I explain the processes of technical change on Corn Belt family farms during the interwar period. Focusing on the farm tractor, I highlight the contingent and contested context for these developments. I then present a class analytical model of these changes, and explain how they were driven in part by competition and the hunt for super profits among ancient farmers. These processes laid the foundation for the modern industrial agricultural system. I examine the contradictory impacts of the hunt for super profits on various participants in the farm economy, and explain how they both resolved and contributed to the farm problem during the interwar period, and set the stage for further development after World War II along with the intensification of the farm problem throughout the remainder of the twentieth century. The section that follows extends the analysis to include the impacts of state policy on the hunt for super profits after 1933. State policy will be shown to further reinforce the path toward the industrialization of agriculture and its accompanying trends toward fewer, larger, more capital-intensive farms, rural depopulation, and the growth of agribusiness.

The tractor dilemma: through the lens of class

In a 1940 report on farm technology, the USDA singled out the two most significant innovations of the century until that time: the farm tractor and hybrid corn (USDA 1940b). "The tractor more than any other force," the report's authors explained, "has brought an industrial revolution to our farms" (USDA 1940b, 9). Farmers began adopting lightweight tractors in large numbers in the 1920s, and hybrid seed in the 1930s.[3] The tractor represented the second phase of a mechanization process for cereal crop production that had begun in the previous century. The first phase involved the introduction of horse-powered farm machinery in place of hand-powered implements, and included innovations like Cyrus McCormick's reaper (1831), John Deere's steel-tipped moldboard plow (1837), and Hiram Moore's combined harvester (1834). These and many other new machines for planting and cultivating came into widespread use in the 1850s, and helped farmers reduce labor costs (particularly in response to labor shortages during and after the Civil War) and increase control of the production process.

The second phase of mechanization was launched with the internal combustion engine and the development of flexible, maneuverable traction – the farm tractor. The first operational gasoline-powered tractor was built in 1892, and Hart and Parr offered the first commercial tractor in 1901. The other major competing source of traction power was horses and mules, which were used for every major task on a farm including tilling, planting, cultivating, mowing and hauling. The number of horses and mules on farms peaked at 27 million in 1917, the same year that Henry Ford introduced the first small, multi-purpose, mass-produced and affordable tractor.[4] The Fordson Model F sold for $750, making it possible for the average farmer to own a tractor for the first time, especially with wartime demand boosting farm receipts. By 1925, Ford had built its 500,000th tractor, but it was soon overshadowed by International Harvester Company, which revolutionized the industry with the introduction of the Farmall in 1924. With its tricycle design wheel arrangement, it was the first low-priced tractor built for row-crop farming because it could maneuver through the rows of growing crops without damaging the plants, and it soon made the Fordson obsolete.

In addition to the tricycle wheel design, other complementary innovations played a significant role in improving the tractor's performance and utility on farms. These included improved oil and air filters, implements, and hitches. The power take-off was added in 1918 so that the tractor could power other machines such as mowers and pickers. Pneumatic rubber tires introduced in 1930 replaced steel wheels and allowed tractors to travel comfortably on roads, reduced vibrations and fuel consumption, and increased durability.

Tractors, along with trucks, combines, and mechanical corn pickers, quickly displaced human and animal power on farms throughout the Corn Belt. Between 1920 and 1930, farms with tractors in Illinois and Iowa, the heart of the Corn Belt, went from 9 to 30 percent (Ankli 1980). The number of tractors on farms increased from 246,000 in 1920 to 920,000 in 1930. Thanks in part to the New Deal agricultural policies enacted in 1933, the latter years of the Depression saw a dramatic recovery in tractor sales after an initial decline during the decade so that, by 1940, tractors on farms had reached 1.56 million (Gardner 2006; Carter et al. 2006) (see Figure 3.2). By 1930, farm power provided by internal combustion engines had surpassed all sources of animal power. Olmstead and Rhode

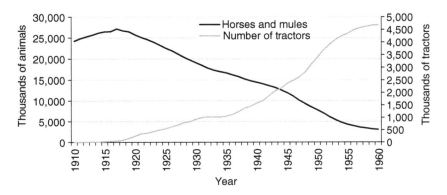

Figure 3.2 Number of animals vs. number of tractors on farms, 1910–1960 (data from Carter, Susan B., Scott Sigmund Gartner, Michael R. Haines, Alan L. Olmstead, Richard Sutch, and Gavin Wright, eds. 2006. *Historical Statistics of the United States, Earliest Times to the Present: Millennial Edition Online.* New York: Cambridge University Press. Available online at http://hsus.cambridge.org/HSUSWeb/HSUSEntryServlet).

suggest that the writing was on the wall for the horse industry by the mid-1920s. Even though horses were still required to complete many tasks on farms, they represented only between 15 and 30 percent of new investments in farm horse-power capacity (Olmstead and Rhode 2001).

While farm mechanization is sometimes presented as the inevitable result of the march of progress, the arrival of the farm tractor was neither inevitable, nor necessarily a harbinger of progress. In part reflecting the uneven distribution of benefits among farmers, rural communities, and businesses, the arrival of the "horseless age" was a hotly contested issue, and its social and economic ramifications were widely debated.[5] "It has been said that the forces of technology cannot be stopped, but they can be directed into more socially desirable channels," asserted the *New York Times*, and then proceeded to pose the difficult question of what exactly those "socially desirable goals" entailed. "Should agriculture strive for maximum efficiency in production with larger and larger units, more concentrated ownership and management, and fewer and fewer farmers?" (*The New York Times* 1937). Secretary of Agriculture, Henry A. Wallace posed the dilemma more starkly in a speech given at Council Bluffs, Iowa: "Shall American agriculture let an uncontrolled technology wipe out the independent family-sized farm, or shall American agriculture turn its back on technology, in order to preserve the family-sized farm?" (*Daily Boston Globe* 1936) How could the seemingly irresistible tractor be luring the family farmer to his demise?

Concern for the impacts of the tractor on farmers, farm structure, and rural communities was widespread, although many viewed these problems as a necessary price to pay for progress. Economist Willford King examined the evidence and found that the tractor, and the gasoline engine in general, was responsible for "the continuance of the farm depression ushered in by the price deflation of 1920." Nevertheless, he thought it beneficial from a "national standpoint" as it probably contributed to a more efficient allocation of resources (King 1929, 72). The Horse Association of America (HAA), founded in 1919, was one of the primary organizations mounting a serious battle on behalf of those with vested business (and other) interests in the horse. The HAA also linked the decline of horses on farms with the farm crisis of the 1920s and 1930s, arguing that tractors were responsible for overproduction, falling prices, and farm bankruptcies. In fact, they claimed that a high percentage of those going bankrupt were tractor users because they had greater exposure to markets, not only in paying for their tractors, loans, and fuel, but also in marketing the increased output the tractors made possible. The HAA also claimed tractors brought with them dependence on distant oil and implement companies, rather than keeping incomes within local communities, and questioned the bias of USDA and university research, as well as farm creditors, toward mechanization. As an example of the bias, and the ways in which expectations about the tractor's triumph became self-fulfilling, bankers responded to perceptions that the horse's days were numbered by refusing to continue accepting horses as collateral for loans. Meanwhile, bankers as well as tractor manufacturers would carry notes for the purchase of a tractor.

Farmers who relied on credit for acquiring new means of production therefore found it easier to purchase a new tractor than a horse.

In a 1937 report, the National Resources Committee, established by FDR to manage the New Deal emergency relief appropriations, warned of the "ever-widening gap between the man with the hoe and the man with the tractor." The uneven impact of the new technology heightened tension among agricultural groups. "Unrestrained competition," warned the committee, "will lead toward greater concentration of commercial production on fewer farms with an increase in the average size of these farms and fewer commercial farmers" (*The New York Times* 1937). Professor Paul S. Taylor, testifying opposite Fowler McCormick, vice president of the International Harvester Company and grandson of Cyrus McCormick before the Temporary National Economic Committee investigating monopoly in 1940 concurred, explaining how "Already we hear half-articulate appeals from distressed and fearful farmers against 'land monopoly,' 'land hogs' and 'tractoring out' " (*The New York Times* 1940a).

Tractor boosters touted the increase in productivity, profitability, and predictability offered by the transition to gasoline power. Advertisements for the Farmall described it as a "Great Emancipator," freeing the farmer from the drudgery of fieldwork, and making him the "master of time and season." International Harvester urged farmers to try out the tractor's greatest asset, its power, and the profits it "produced." On advertisement advised, "[R]esolve to be the master of mechanical power." (Clarke 2002, 84–88). Reliable and steady, unlike work animals, the tractor never needed time off for rest, or care when idle, and could work through heat, insects, and hard ground. In his 1940 testimony, McCormick explained the many benefits of the tractor for farmers, including not only the relief from drudgery, but also the increased profit "by supplying speedier methods of evading the hazards of weather." McCormick assured the Congressional committee that tractors "promised to preserve the family-operated farm as an American institution" (*The New York Times* 1940a).

In Marxian terms, the purchase of a tractor offered the early-adopting ancient farmers the possibility of capturing "super profits" from laggard competitors by improving labor productivity and lowering their unit costs of production (Resnick 2006). See Appendix A for numerical examples illustrating the following arguments. If we assume again the simplified situation in which the ancient farmer labored by himself in the family farm enterprise, then the non-class revenue flow of super profits supplemented the surplus produced by the ancient farmer, providing for expanded ancient subsumed class distributions.[6]

Farmers who adopted the tractor could increase labor productivity, producing the same amount of use values (bushels of corn) in less time. Or, as Marx explained it, "The exceptionally productive labour operates as intensified labour; it creates in equal periods of time greater values than average social labour of the same kind" (Marx 1975, 302). Not only did this free up a farmer's time to cultivate more acreage (if he had access to the additional land), but it also meant he could cultivate his existing acreage more efficiently. For example, one of the most arduous but urgent tasks on the farm was spring plowing, and it often required extra horses to complete. Either a farmer had to keep extra horses for the entire year, or gain access to extras at this time. Overcoming the springtime bottleneck and completing the plowing in a timely manner could make the difference between a successful crop and a failure. For example, one study found that delaying springtime planting (which could only be done after plowing) by just 10 days reduced yields in Illinois by three bushels per acre (Ankli 1980, 139). Average yield at the time was approximately 50 bushels per acre.

A single horse required 10 hours to break one acre, and a large team of six horses could plow only six acres in a day. The standard 10 horsepower tractor could plow approximately 10 acres in a 10 hour day. Ankli estimated that for all the different steps of corn production a tractor saved approximately seven man hours per acre compared to large team, and 24 man hours per acre compared to a small team (three to four horses). Thus, for a farm with 40 acres of corn, the tractor could save, at minimum, roughly 280 hours, or nearly a month of work (and this did not even include the time required to raise oats and hay to feed the horse teams) (Ankli 1980).

The tractor also increased a farmer's effective land base, without necessitating increased subsumed class payments for ground rent. Even though most farms continued to rely on both horses and tractors until after World War II, a tractor still replaced an average of two to three horses per farm (Clarke 2002; Hurt 2003). Tractors could replace the otherwise unneeded horses the farmer kept for plowing and disking in the spring, but farmers still preferred to rely on horses for planting and cultivating (Reynoldson 1922). According to International Harvester, the number of completely horseless farms numbered only 1,000 out of more than six million in 1929 (Clarke 2002). A farmer gained three to five acres of cropland and pasture from producing feed and fodder for every horse replaced by a tractor. Thus, the farmer with a tractor had not only the capacity to farm more acres more quickly, but also the additional acres available, further increasing the bushels of corn (use values) produced.

In Marxian value terms, average costs per bushel of corn are expressed as follows: (C+V)/UV (where C is ancient constant capital, V is ancient variable capital, and UV is number of use values). While the tractor clearly increased UV in the denominator for a given V, or reduced V for a given UV, it probably increased the magnitude of C, including both fixed and circulating capital. Even if it did not increase the magnitude of C, the tractor increased the cash portion of constant capital. Since most farmers did not value either non-purchased labor or capital at market rates, this increase in cash costs amounted to the same thing as an increase in costs as a whole (Clarke 2002). Tractors required larger initial outlays than a team of horses, and taking full advantage of their potential required purchasing additional equipment as well, including a plow, disk, planter, and cultivator. For example, in 1929, a tractor cost around $1,000 while a team of six horses cost an average of $474 ($79 per horse) (Clarke 2002). The depreciation cost of the fixed capital was the largest component of a tractor's costs. In addition, the purchase of a tractor required additional cash outlays for circulating capital including fuel, oil, and grease, as well as maintenance and repair (if the latter were purchased as well). If tractors replaced draft animals, they may have also entailed increased costs for purchased fertilizers. Finally, the purchase of a tractor often required access to credit, and hence a new subsumed class payment for interest on the loan (Clarke 2002; Macy 1938, 58).

Because a tractor represented an increase in fixed capital costs, and in cash fixed and circulating capital costs, farmers of larger farms were more likely to experience a reduction in average costs and therefore to purchase a tractor (Ankli 1980; Olmstead and Rhode 2001). Clarke estimated that at least 100 acres was needed to make the tractor cost effective for Corn Belt farms in 1929 (2002, 93). While most (72 percent) of farms in Iowa were more than 100 acres, only 45 percent of farms were larger in Indiana. For larger ancient farmers, the savings could be substantial, however. International Harvester featured one such farmer, Mr. Elza C. Lawson of Illinois in one of its advertisements. Lawson's costs per bushel of corn with a tractor on his 100 acres of the crop were 14.5 cents, compared to the official government estimate of 32.66 cents per bushel in the Midwest (or $7.25 per acre versus $16.33 at 50 bushels per acre) (Clarke 2002, 83). Since farmers usually planted about two-thirds of their land in crops, Lawson's farm was well over the 100 acre threshold.

Farmers like Lawson who purchased tractors during the early period in the 1920s were able to boost productivity, thereby lowering average costs below those of their competitors and reducing the private labor time necessary to produce corn on their farms. Because all farmers sold at the same socially determined market price (exchange value per unit), those with lower unit costs gained a "super profit," or a share of the surplus produced in the less productive enterprises, but realized by the lower-cost innovators. The private actions of innovating farmers were transmitted to others through market exchange processes, lowering the social average unit value, and therefore the market price of corn.[7] More efficient farmers realized more revenue in exchange than was expected in production because their actions drove a wedge between the social and private unit value of corn. The difference, or super profit, was therefore equal to the difference between the social unit value faced in the market and the private unit value multiplied by the bushels of corn sold.[8]

The additional surplus captured by innovating farmers placed them in a superior position to grow their enterprises, by gaining access to further productivity-enhancing inputs and the technologies they embodied, by acquiring land, or by acquiring the credit for these purchases. Acquisition of new chemical, biological, or mechanical equipment was important because these innovations were often synergistic. For example, while it was initially thought that farmers could utilize horse-drawn equipment with their new tractors, it soon became evident that the old equipment was not sufficient. If a plow became stuck in the field it would break under the increased drawbar power of the tractor as opposed to the horses which would automatically stop when stuck. Spending an additional $200 to $300 on new implements was therefore common. An additional problem created by the tractor was that of fertility. Since horses and mules on farms provided not only traction power but also fertility, replacing them created the need for farmers to turn increasingly to outside sources for fertility, and as they did so the commercial fertilizer market began expanding, beginning in the late 1920s. In fact, the most rapid growth of the industry, after WWII, coincided with the rapid increase in the number of completely horseless farms (among other things). In the 1930s, the tractor facilitated the adoption of hybrid corn, and vice versa. Hybrids were more uniform and their stronger stalks were resistant to lodging (falling down), facilitating mechanical harvesting. In addition, they could be planted more densely (an important source of their increased yields), which required a tractor rather than the wider spacing required for horses to work in the fields. Thus, super profits provided a means for innovators to further outpace their competitors through productivity-enhancing ancient accumulation, thereby continually lowering costs of production and gaining further super profits.

Acquisition of land was especially important because it meant a further reduction in average costs as the tractor's fixed expenses could be spread over a larger production. Not only were more educated farmers of large farms more likely to purchase a tractor, but farms had a tendency to get larger as a result. Prosperous farmers were well-positioned to take advantage of the tractor's benefits in the first place, and the consequences reinforced their lead. Evidence seems to indicate that it was not for the most part small and medium-sized farmers who reaped the benefits of mechanization and were able to expand as a result, but rather the already large farmers who were able to pay the costs of mechanization and hence, also to gain the super profits (Garkovich and Bokemeier 1988, 221). A variety of USDA and experiment station studies at the time showed that farmers increased acreage and changed cropping patterns after acquiring a tractor. A 1916 study of Illinois farms found that about one third of tractor owners who stated that tractors were profitable increased the acreage they were farming, by an average of 120 acres per farm (Olmstead and Rhode 2001). Tractors and the income they generated also helped farmers gain access to credit, which was often needed to finance the purchase of land and other equipment. For example, as previously discussed, by the 1920s, banks accepted tractors as collateral for loans, and farm implement dealers regularly extended credit for the purchase as well. Horses, however, were no longer accepted in securing loans (Olmstead and Rhode 1994).

Obtaining, keeping, and expanding super profits, however, created a contradictory situation for all farmers, even for the early-bird innovators. They faced the possibility of a variety of new claims on their surplus in the form of one or more subsumed class payments for rent, additional means of production, and interest. Not only were these new claims on the surplus, but they were mostly new *cash* claims on the surplus of innovating farmers. New inputs often replaced those previously produced by the farmer himself, including traction power, fodder, feed, seed, and fertilizer. The shift from produced to purchased C-goods, with the accompanying cash payments, constituted a dramatic change in the nature of farming costs, exposing farmers and their families to market risk to an extent that many had not hitherto experienced. For example, in 1929, Midwestern farmers spent an average of $1,220 in cash outlays for annual farm expenses.

The purchase of a $1,000 tractor therefore constituted a significant increase in cash outlays. Even if the purchase were financed, long term credit was scarce so the loan was likely to require relatively rapid repayment (Clarke 2002).

The relationships between the farm enterprise and the farm household, and between the hybrid class structures within the family farm, were altered accordingly. For example, helping out directly in farm production became less necessary, while making do was more so, in order to save or generate more cash for the purchase and upkeep of the new equipment. In addition, added cash expenditures increased the need to keep track of farm accounts, an activity which farm women often took over, thus increasing the labor time they expended on this subsumed class activity (Garkovich and Bokemeier 1988, 223; Neth 1998). These changes are discussed further below.

While innovating farmers faced a contradictory situation – increased surplus realized, along with increased claims on that surplus, as well as increased exposure to a decline in cash earnings – others faced an unmistakable crisis. Innovators gained at the direct expense of others. Unless the laggard farmer's labor was of industry average productivity (producing zero super profit), his surplus was being siphoned away. Because the innovating farmer pulled down the average unit value of corn, the laggard found that his private unit value exceeded the market price/social unit value. In this case, he was in effect paying for the use of the market, in the form of lower-than-expected revenues realized, or a negative super profit. What he lost in his encounter with the exchange process, his tractor-farming neighbor gained. Since the private unit value exceeded the market exchange value, super profits were negative. Assuming the horse-farming ancient farmer's revenues and expenditures were initially in balance, he now faced a class crisis. The revenues he realized were no longer sufficient to cover the necessary subsumed class payments to secure his conditions of existence. As *The New York Times* put it in a 1937 headline: "Man with the Hoe Losing to Tractor."

Laggard farmers were forced to respond in some way, or else risk death as an ancient farmer and the loss of land to an innovating neighbor seeking to expand. Indeed, evidence suggests that increasing numbers of farmers either chose or were forced onto this path. Stable acreage under cultivation along with an increase in the acreage per farm required it (King 1929). Even though the post-War crisis was severe, it was short-lived, and relatively localized. Yet farm bankruptcy rates continued to increase throughout the decade from less than four in one thousand before the war, to 11 between 1921 and 1925, and to seventeen in the late 1920s (Clarke 2002). Indeed, census numbers bear out what many observers began noticing at the time: the number of farmers was declining. More than a quarter of a million farmers abandoned their farms for the cities during the 1920s (King 1929, 69). Since the ratio of workers (family and hired) to farms was about two, this means there was an explosion in the relative surplus population in the countryside leading to a massive structural shift in the U.S. population. The USDA estimated that in 1944, the tractor saved roughly 1.7 billion man-hours per year in field work and caring for draft animals relative to the 1917 to 1921 period. Olmstead and Rhode estimate that this translated into approximately 850,000 workers (Olmstead and Rhode 2001, 665). While the Great Depression interrupted this trend as many of the unemployed from the cities made their way back to the farms, swelling the ranks of the rural population, the trend toward mass rural to urban migration continued and accelerated after World War II.

Differently situated and differently impacted farmers pursued a variety of other strategies to stay in the farming game. In his discussion of super profits, Marx focused on one possible strategy – that of imitation and diffusion of the new technology. "The law of the determination of value by labour-time, acting as a coercive law of competition, forces [the innovator's] competitors to adopt the new method" (Marx 1975; 302). Processes of technical change shaped the competitive environment, and vice versa, intensifying competition among ancient farmers and stimulating further rounds of technical change and diffusion. Many rushed to follow the innovator's lead by purchasing a new tractor. As early tractor models steadily improved, second-movers may even have gained an advantage over the early adopters, erasing their super profits and gaining their own from them. This process contributed to stimulating further purchases of new and improved tractors and other implements as innovators fought the onslaught by seeking to lower average costs further. Figures on new tractor manufacturing and farmer purchases suggest there was a high rate of discard and re-purchase, and consequently a short life-span for early models (Martini 2003). In addition, the price of a tractor steadily declined (or remained stable in spite of improvements) throughout the 1920s, allowing more farmers to jump into the fray.[9] For example, Ford slashed the price of the Fordson to $395 in January 1922 (Ankli 1980; Olmstead and Rhode 2001). This suggests that tractor farmers were leapfrogging each other with each new tractor purchase as models steadily improved and grew cheaper.[10]

The process of diffusion unleashed contradictory processes that undermined all farmers' profitability, however. The increase in the productivity of abstract labor in corn production forced the unit value of corn constantly downward, erasing or redistributing gains and losses from the hunt for super profits (even as subsumed class claims in the form of ground rent and interest payments increased). The increase in the organic composition of capital as the proportion of C-goods in total costs rose contributed to a falling value rate of profit in corn farming. That is, as $C/(C+V)$ increased, $S/(C+V)$ declined (where C stands for ancient constant capital, V for ancient variable capital, and S for ancient surplus).

The widespread adoption of productivity-enhancing technologies boosted the supply of corn (and other farm commodities). Just the decline in horses and mules on farms of roughly 6.6 million during the 1920s freed up between 20 and 33 million acres of land for food production. The USDA estimated that between 1915 and 1930, the 10 million horses and mules displaced from farms released 30 million acres of cropland and 15 million acres of pasture (USDA 1940a). By 1960, the number had climbed to roughly 60 million acres of cropland, or an area roughly equal to "two-thirds of the total cropland harvested in 1920 in the territory of the Louisiana Purchase" (Olmstead and Rhode 2001, 665). Combined with the increased yields per acre, the tractor brought an immense shift in cropping patterns toward the production of food crops like corn. Observers at this time began to speak of "structural oversupply" and its accompanying problems.

This increased supply forced the market price of corn constantly downward as well. Since the demand for many farm commodities, including corn, cotton, wheat, and potatoes, was inelastic during this period, even small increases in supply could have larger relative impacts on price. The increased supply of corn could have forced corn prices below unit values, creating a negative non-class revenue due to unequal exchange for every farmer using markets. Even if this did not occur, the stage was set for a further round of technical change, crisis, and response in a process of "immiserizing growth" that agricultural historian Willard Cochrane called "the technology treadmill" (Cochrane 1993). Once farmers began climbing on the treadmill in the 1920s, they found it difficult to get off unscathed.

From the 1920s, the treadmill steadily gained speed, throwing off millions of farmers who could no longer afford to keep up as they incurred debt and new claims on their surplus. Even though the index of prices received by farmers reached 148 in 1929 on the eve of the Great Depression (compared to the Golden Age period of 1909 to 1914), the parity ratio between prices received and prices paid by farmers had fallen to 92 by 1929, indicating that farmers continued to suffer a cost-price squeeze as agricultural prices received lagged behind costs[11] (see Figure 3.3). Declining profits in spite of seemingly unending work drove

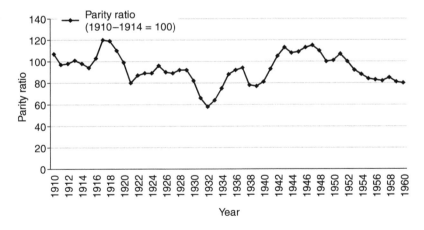

Figure 3.3 Parity ratio: prices received/prices paid by farmers, 1910–1960 (data from Carter, Susan B., Scott Sigmund Gartner, Michael R. Haines, Alan L. Olmstead, Richard Sutch, and Gavin Wright, eds. 2006. *Historical Statistics of the United States, Earliest Times to the Present: Millennial Edition Online*. New York: Cambridge University Press. Available online at http://hsus.cambridge.org/HSUSWeb/HSUSEntryServlet).

farmers and their families from rural areas. By 1929, the rural population had declined by almost two million from its 1916 peak of 32.5 million (Hurt 2003, 46).

On the other hand, the technology treadmill set in motion processes that tended to offset the decline in the value profit rate by cheapening the wage good, food. At the time, corn usually made its way into the food supply as feed for hogs and beef cattle. Thus, a cheapening of the price and value of corn meant cheaper food for the population, including workers in farm implement factories, feudal farm family workers, and ancient farmers themselves. The lowered value of ancient and other labor power (V-goods) enabled by the process of technical change in corn production worked to offset the rise in the organic composition of capital by increasing relative surplus value, and contributing toward the cheapening of C-goods as well.

This point was not lost on supporters of either side of the tractor controversy. Tractor boosters played on concerns about food shortages stemming from World War I by posing the choice about mechanization as between "raising horses or feeding humanity" (Olmstead and Rhode 1994). They pointed out that tractors reduced labor costs and therefore food prices, benefitting everyone, especially the poor, and boosting the incomes available to purchase industrial products. These newly prosperous industries would expand, providing employment for displaced farmers and farm workers. In fact, the people joining the ranks of the newly land-less and unemployed weren't so much displaced, as they were newly-freed. Marx would have admired the turn of phrase: "The gasoline engine has released a considerable proportion of our population from agricultural work and has enabled them to produce articles which, for the moment, are in greater demand than are farm products" (King 1929, 70). In Marxian terms, they hoped for a rising real wage along with a declining value of labor power and rising rate of exploitation throughout the economy, enabled by the cheaper food commodities and the accompanying devastation of family farms. Thus, the technology treadmill was churning out the steady supply of cheap workers and cheap food (along with a bonus of demand for industrial products in the process) that had long concerned policymakers and others with which I began this story in Chapter 1.

State policy and the technology treadmill

The importance of agricultural development – of a particular kind and for the benefit of particular interests – helped shape the context for state intervention in the agricultural economy. Faced with a technology-induced class crisis, farmers and farm interests mobilized politically to press the state for policies to address the crisis. This meant overcoming the powerful industrial interests that had pre-vailed through the hard decade of the 1920s in resisting any measure that would increase food prices and, thereby, raw materials costs and wage demands. As discussed above, the Farm Bureau formed in 1920, and proceeded to consolidate support throughout the decade, aided by the formation of the bipartisan Farm Bloc in Congress in 1921. (The Farm Bureau was there to address its first meeting.) By the mid-1920s, support began to coalesce around government intervention to support "equality for agriculture" by supporting farm incomes and prices at an "equitable" level, especially as recognition spread that the situation was more than temporary. As Farm Bureau president, Sam H. Thompson put it, "Farm relief is not any longer considered an emergency matter. The foremost subject, in the mind of agriculture and in the minds of the business people today, is that of proper adjustment of the agricultural industry in our economic life" (*The New York Times* 1926).

On the eve of FDR's inauguration, the farm lobby was recognized as "the most powerful single-industry lobby in Washington" (Hurt 2003). Even then, the term "single-industry" was misleading, as the farm lobby encompassed both much more and much less than the industry of farming itself. Agricultural policy had become the domain of farm implement dealers, fertilizer manufacturers, seed companies, and other agribusiness concerns, farm creditors, land grant universities, state and county extension agents, and USDA officials, to name a few, and of course, farmers, farm families, and rural communities. At the same time, the Farm Bureau, with its membership of the largest, commercially-oriented, prosperous farmers, dominated other farmers' groups. It is certainly true that the configuration of Congressional districts undoubtedly gave (and continues to give) disproportionate weight to the interests of farmers in federal politics, nevertheless it is important to remember that the industry constituted a powerful and far-flung configuration of interests converging around support for government aid to farmers and the continuation of the technology treadmill.

What follows is a class analysis of those policies and the associated ramifications for these various stakeholders in the farm economy, including farm family members. State policy, motivated by the farm crisis shaped the impacts of technical change and competition among ancient farmers from the 1930s onward. State policy resolved the immediate problem of crisis for particular farmers while producing contradictory impacts for all those with a stake in the agricultural economy, including farmers, farm women and children, agribusinesses, and the state itself. State policies helped shape the direction of agricultural development, technical change, and competition after 1935.

Between 1929 and 1932, the Age of Uncertainty had become the Great Depression, and the already limping agricultural economy was utterly hobbled. Farmers faced a realization crisis as prices fell below unit values. For example, the average price of corn fell from 80 cents to 32 cents per bushel. In Iowa, prices were as low as eight to ten cents per bushel. In South Dakota, corn prices fell as low as minus three cents. The terms of trade, as measured by the parity ratio, declined from 92 to 58, and net farm income fell by 67 percent (Carter et al. 2006; Gardner 2006). Farm failure rates increased from 17 to approximately 38 in 1,000. Almost 4 percent of all farms in the United States failed in 1932. Farmers were unable to resolve the crisis themselves, in spite of efforts by the Hoover administration to encourage farmers to produce less. Instead, they responded to collapsing prices by producing more. By Roosevelt's inauguration in early 1933, farmers faced the worst economic situation they had confronted since the 1890s (Hurt 2003, 63–66).

The crisis provided the momentum to propel federal agricultural policy in a new direction under Secretary of Agriculture Henry A. Wallace.[12] Farmers, their creditors, and other agricultural business interests meeting in 1933 agreed that dealing with the crisis required addressing the twin problems of restoring commodity prices and reducing the size of farmers' outstanding debts, and that neither of these things could be accomplished by private individuals alone. There was widespread consensus that the federal government was needed to step in and provide the institutions to correct for the failure of private markets in agriculture (Clarke 2002; Hurt 2003). Doing so would strengthen capitalist industry, as well as large-scale, ancient commercial farmers who were well-represented by the bipartisan Farm Bloc in Congress.

Federal officials argued that intervention was not about boosting a single industry. Rather, a strong agricultural economy was necessary to address the nationwide crisis. Restoring farmers' purchasing power would provide demand to pull industry out of the Depression, as well as to help stem the "backward" flow of the unemployed migrating to the countryside from urban areas. As Wallace explained the day after Roosevelt signed the new legislation, "The new Farm Act ... initiates a program for a general advance of buying power. It is not an isolated advance in a restricted sector; it is part of a large attack on the whole problem of Depression" (Wallace 1932). Although these measures were initially intended to be temporary responses to the emergency, they quickly became the entrenched objects of class and non-class struggle. The policies established during the Roosevelt administration became the basis for the federal government's response to the "farm problem" for the next eighty years. Through these policies, the federal government offered, and has continued to offer, more direct economic assistance to farmers than to any other economic group in the country, an astounding situation given the dramatic shift in the role of farming in the broader economy since the 1930s.

New Deal legislation passed in 1933 created three new federal agencies to deal with the farm crisis, and to help close the gap between required payments and available surplus in farm production in order to ensure the reproduction of ancient farm enterprises and rural communities. These were the Agricultural Adjustment Administration (AAA), the Commodity Credit Corporation (CCC), and the Farm Credit Administration (FCA). AAA and CCC operations mainly worked to establish a new cash revenue position for farmers, while the FCA provided subsidized long term credit.

The AAA targeted seven commodities that were already in surplus: wheat, corn, cotton, rice, tobacco, hogs, and dairy production. It aimed to raise farmers' income by reducing production of these crops, thereby raising their prices to 1910–1914 parity levels. Farmers made land idle by, in essence, renting it to the government at a price per bushel of the crop normally grown there. Payments were calculated on the basis of average yields during a specified previous time period, and the number of acres enrolled. The AAA "policy of scarcity" drew considerable criticism as the production controls instituted midway through the crop year in 1933 resulted in scenes of farmers slaughtering millions of piglets and plowing under crops while growing numbers of Americans suffered from malnutrition and hunger. The AAA was declared unconstitutional in 1936, but production controls continued as a focal point of farm policy, as did the aim of achieving "fair exchange value" or "a fair share of national income."

The CCC operated in conjunction with the AAA in establishing an "ever normal granary" to stabilize commodity prices. Farmers could participate in CCC price support activities only if they also agreed to production controls. In an attempt to counter the bad press associated with the production controls, Wallace referred to the twin pronged approach as "storing the grain in the soil" and "storing it in the bin." Initially corn and cotton were the covered crops, but the popular program soon expanded to other commodities. The CCC was (and still is) a government-owned enterprise responsible for managing the acquisition, storage, and sale of surplus crops. CCC price supports took the form of a nonrecourse loan with the crop pledged as collateral. Corn producers, for example, could obtain a loan at the "fair exchange value," called the loan rate, for every bushel of corn sealed in storage. If the market price rose above the loan rate, the farmer could sell the corn, repay the loan, and retain the net proceeds, thus benefiting from the higher prices. If the market price remained below the loan rate, however, the farmer could default on the loan, forfeiting the crop in payment of the debt, thus limiting losses to no more than the initial debt (in the upper limit case that the market price matched the loan rate). Loans were extended at very low interest rates, at or near CCC borrowing rates from the U.S. Treasury. Corn was mostly stored by the farmers themselves with government verification, while other crops were stored in public facilities.

Signaling the significance of this unprecedented intervention in the agricultural economy, the occasion of the first corn loan was the subject of an extensive article and full page of photographs published in *The Des Moines Register* depicting Mr. W. Eral of Pocahontas, Iowa, the first farmer to receive a corn loan under the new program. Mr. Eral received $585, or 45 cents a bushel for his 1,300 bushels of corn placed in storage (a crop which the previous year had been worth a mere eight to ten cents per bushel), and the promise to reduce his planted acreage during the next crop year (1933). The success of the CCC in modulating corn prices after the drought of 1934, along with the sustained positive press given to the program succeeded in garnering widespread support. By 1937, the CCC had become the principal means of supporting farm prices.

The AAA and CCC attempted to address the problem of stabilizing farm incomes and commodity prices, thus boosting farmers' ability to repay their debts and stemming the tide of foreclosures that followed in the wake of depressed commodity prices in 1933. The FCA tackled the issue of the supply of credit to match the revenue and expenditure cycles of most farmers. Existing sources of credit were mostly short term, while farmers often required intermediate term loans between planting and harvest, or long term loans for land or equipment. Further, deposits at local banks often fluctuated with farm prices and incomes, meaning rural banks were least able to offer loans in years when farmers most needed them. Through the FCA, the government became the chief financing agent for farmers, purchasing and refinancing mortgages, extending short and intermediate loan facilities, and lowering interest rates. Farm foreclosures decreased dramatically after peaking in 1933, as both outstanding farm debt and interest payments fell. By 1937, the FCA held 40 percent of all farm mortgages, and had become the most important agency for supplying farmers' credit needs. The FCA also presented competition for private lenders, who soon began offering longer term loan products and lower rates in response.

The farm crisis situation suggests that a growing number of farmers were subject to the possibility of a persistent and growing gap between revenues and expenditures. Government measures attempted to resolve the farm crisis. They worked on the shortfall between the ancient farmer's revenues and expenditures by either increasing ancient revenues or reducing ancient subsumed class payments. Government payments also increased the cash component of any revenues. Increased revenues meant increasing ancient surplus and/or establishing a new non-class revenue position for ancient farmers. Decreasing expenditures meant reducing the number and/or magnitude of ancient subsumed class payments.[13] Government farm programs generally impacted ancient surplus only indirectly, and impacted farmers directly by establishing a series of new non-class revenues from the state, as well as reducing the number and magnitude of subsumed class payments by providing a variety of ancient conditions of existence that the private sector was unwilling or unable to provide, at reduced or even zero cost to farmers.

AAA production controls encouraged farmers to store their corn "in the soil" by, in effect, renting a portion of a farmer's land in exchange for a non-class revenue payment.[14] Significantly, production controls were instituted through acreage allotment plans, not by direct marketing quotas. Thus, enterprising farmers could subvert production controls by increasing output per acre on non-idle land. Wealthy farmers with large holdings were more likely to be able to purchase access to the new technologies like tractors available to do this. Under this scheme, the more acres a farmer had to enroll in the program, and the more productive those acres, the higher the payments. The AAA both encouraged and enabled mechanization because farmers had both an incentive and also a new source of cash revenue at their disposal to purchase new equipment.

In addition, the program rewarded land ownership more than land tenancy, since landowners were not obligated to share their benefit checks with tenants, and acreage reductions meant fewer tenants.[15] Landowners could evict tenants, and continue to collect AAA checks on the basis of their tenants' past labor in production. If the landowner were also the farmer of the idled land, he would have occupied both the position of landlord and of farmer, and the state rental payments would, in effect, have replaced the subsumed class revenue for rent that he might have previously distributed to himself in exchange for the subsumed class service of access to his land. Instead of either paying himself, or providing the access for free, the federal government made an explicit cash payment approximately equal to the "opportunity cost" of the idle acres.

CCC operations addressed the realization crisis for farmers, with the government acting as merchant and financier as needed, thereby reversing what had become a negative non-class revenue position due to plummeting prices (below unit values) and surplus crops. The program established a new revenue position for farmers producing supported commodities that varied with the units of the commodity produced and placed in storage, as well as with the difference between the "fair market value" or loan rate, and the market price. The "fair market value" was expressed as a percentage of 1909–1914 parity. If the price support were operational, that is the loan rate was above the market price, the farmer in effect took a loan, or advance payment for his crop, at the loan rate per unit of commodity placed in storage, but paid it back at the lower market rate per unit of commodity placed in storage by "selling" his stored commodity to the federal government. If the loan rate were below the market price, the farmer in effect took a loan valued at the loan rate per unit of commodity placed in storage, and paid it back at the same rate per unit of commodity placed in storage, but sold his commodity at the higher market price, and pocketed the difference between the market price and the loan rate.[16]

Once again, farmers who produced more and placed more in storage could receive larger payments. Also notable was that if the market price were below the loan rate, the burden of the payment fell on the government, which also incurred the cost of storing and later marketing the forfeited crops. If the opposite were true, the cost was born by private buyers of the commodity. Theoretically, the CCC loan and storage operations were supposed to operate to keep the market price hovering around the loan rate, hence the term "ever normal granary." If it went above, the CCC could release some of its stores on the market to lower the price. If it went below, the CCC would withhold the forfeited crops from the market to raise the price. The loan rate therefore served as an anchor around which the market price of supported commodities was to fluctuate, with the farmer gaining no matter whether it was over or under, and the government incurring added costs only if it were under. Combined with acreage allotments to control the supply, the programs together were supposed to minimize government expenditures. In practice, the "ever normal granary" combined with acreage allotments encouraged farmers to increase productivity on their active acreage, thereby subverting acreage controls.

In addition to the cash non-class revenues provided through the new programs, the FCA provided the subsumed class service of access to the kinds of loans that had not been previously available to farmers and at reduced cost. Farmers thus not only enjoyed expanded access to intermediate and long term credit, but also a reduced subsumed class payment in exchange for that access.

The New Deal farm programs may not have been sufficient to jolt the economy out of the Great Depression, but they were nevertheless effective in restarting, and even intensifying, the technology treadmill. Price supports, however, shifted its contradictory consequences. In particular, the adoption and widespread imitation of new technologies, making farmers more efficient, did not result in a falling value rate of profit in the same way. The resolution of this particular contradiction nevertheless gave rise to still others, and helps explain notable features of subsequent U.S. agricultural development. These included rapid technical change and the industrialization of farm production, the rise of agribusiness, the contentious continuation of farm programs, and chronic crisis along with a radical restructuring among farmers. These developments, along with their differential class consequences are discussed further below. First, I examine the hunt for super profits in the context of state price supports for farm commodities.

Just as before government intervention to support prices, the adoption and diffusion of productivity-enhancing technologies resulted in the decline in average costs and unit value per bushel (see Appendix A for numerical examples illustrating the discussion that follows). However, government-supported prices did not automatically fall (although because they became increasingly expensive to maintain, political pressure mounted to lower them). As before, the farmer who innovated first lowered his private unit value below the social average, capturing a super profit from his competitors. Also as before, the innovator's newly-lowered private unit value pulled the social average value down. If we assume that the government-supported fair market value was initially equal to the social average unit value before innovation, then in the context of government-supported prices at "fair market value," the following new situation arose. The government-supported price was now greater than the social average unit value, and the social average unit value was greater than the private unit value for innovators. For non-innovators, the private unit value was equal to the government-supported price, both of which were greater than the social average unit value. The hunt for super profits in the context of government price supports drove a wedge not only between the private and social unit values, but also between the social unit value and the price farmers received. Due to government price supports, the price remained above the social unit value, generating additional non-class revenue for both innovators and laggards.[17] Government price supports encouraged farmers to undertake actions (the purchase of a tractor or other innovation), that lowered the exchange value of corn but not the government-determined fair market value, the price that farmers received for the corn they produced and stored.

Innovating farmers received positive super profits because their labor was of higher than average productivity. This non-class revenue constituted a transfer from less productive ancient farmers. In addition, the innovating farmers received the non-class revenue payment from the state, to make up the difference between the unit exchange value and the fair market value that farmers received. Farmers whose labor was of lower than average productivity suffered a negative super profit, a transfer of value produced by them, but realized by their innovating competitors. The loss they suffered, however, was in this case exactly offset by the transfer from the state, which they also received, for each and every bushel of corn that was subject to the price support.[18]

The relative distance between innovators and laggards still existed. The innovating farmer was still in a superior position to grow his enterprise, thereby intensifying competition, and forcing others to respond to his private actions. On the other hand, this competition played out differently than if farmers were subject to the declining market prices instigated by their actions. As noted above, one possible response was to imitate the innovating farmer, and purchase the new tractor or other inputs, which many farmers did. Pursuing this strategy, however, no longer produced the same contradictory consequences of falling prices and unit values due to expanding supply and increased productivity. Instead, prices did not fall, and farmers as a group now had *nothing to lose* by following the leading innovator. Initially, at least, farmers appeared to have escaped the contradictory consequence of a falling rate of profit accompanying their otherwise successful innovating actions. A rising organic composition of capital, along with a rising rate and mass of profits in corn production, was financed by state expenditures.

Evidence suggests that farm policies were an important factor in shifting the subsequent trajectory of agricultural development, as predicted by the model. The first government checks went out to farmers in the fall of 1933, and purchases of tractors picked up soon thereafter. By 1935, the leading tractor manufacturer, International Harvester was so far back in the black after experiencing its first losses in its history in 1932 and 1933, that it advised farmers, "If you'll need a tractor in 1936 you ought to order it now" (Clarke 2002, 162). According to the advertisement, the company simply could not keep up with the surprising flood of orders in 1935. The number of farms owning tractors in the Midwest increased from 25 to 42 percent. Tractor sales more than doubled between 1933 and 1934 from 25,000 to 65,000, then nearly doubled again in 1935 to 122,000 (see Figure 3.4). In addition to tractors, farmers increased purchases of hybrid corn, exploiting synergies between the two technologies. From less than 1 percent of planted acreage in 1933, hybrids spread to 90 percent of corn acreage by 1945 (Fitzgerald 1993, 340). As farms moved away from producing fodder and un-supported crops and toward monoculture from the highly diversified farming systems, reduced species diversity on farms required the increasing use of chemicals to control weeds and insects.

Altogether, the new farm policies dramatically altered the balance of relationships in which ancient farmers were engaged. Access to credit lowered the cost to farmers of long-term investment decisions. In addition, the government now provided the important condition of existence of price and income stability, shouldering some of the risk in a risky occupation, and especially controlling the risk associated with taking on cash commitments. By providing farmers guaranteed cash income, farm policies changed the decision-making environment for ancient farmers, and encouraged them to borrow and buy new machinery and land, and to shift from non-monetary to monetary costs of production (Clarke 2002). Farmers increasingly turned to credit and input markets to complete their production processes. In addition, they increasingly specialized in supported crops, in part because the complex art of diversification to reduce risk was no longer as necessary.

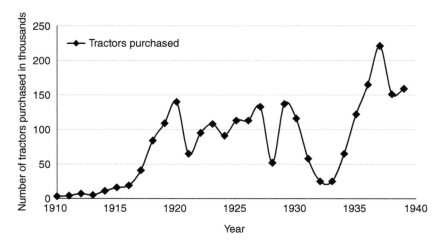

Figure 3.4 Tractors purchased by year, 1910–1940 (data from Carter, Susan B., Scott
Sigmund Gartner, Michael R. Haines, Alan L. Olmstead, Richard Sutch, and
Gavin Wright, eds. 2006. *Historical Statistics of the United States, Earliest
Times to the Present: Millennial Edition Online.* New York: Cambridge Uni-
versity Press. Available online at http://hsus.cambridge.org/HSUSWeb/
HSUSEntryServlet).

These policies served to focus and magnify the workings of the hunt for super
profits and its accompanying ramifications. Wallace himself spoke about the
impacts of new technologies on the farm economy on several occasions, noting
that technical change tended to benefit the more prosperous farmers:

> On the whole, it seems clear that in industry as in agriculture a rather high
> percentage of the benefits of increased productivity, resulting from new
> inventions and new methods, goes to the people who are better off. There
> are plenty of exceptions, but on the whole technology exalts the dominance
> of those already on top and makes more hopeless the position of those at the
> bottom of the pile.

(Wallace 1937)

Farm programs channeled farmers further down the path of mechanization and
industrialization, rewarding larger, capital-intensive farmers who borrowed to
finance the purchase of new machinery to improve per acre productivity, and
then used their resulting super profits to buy the land of their less fortunate
neighbors. The federal government threw its resources behind the aim of helping
already prosperous farmers become more so. Sharecroppers, tenants, and low-
income farmers were virtually ignored, as they were considered too poor, ineffi-
cient, and/or backward to benefit from government assistance. Wallace solidified
this policy direction in 1935, when he fired the "radicals" in the department who

supported policy actions to distribute the benefits of agricultural policies more broadly (Hurt 2003, 74; Jellison 1993).

Policies promoting technical change to increase productivity might seem to conflict with production control measures, but not if we consider that USDA policies were not meant to help all farmers. They were meant to restart the technology treadmill after the disastrous crash, and in fact they did so. From this perspective, the farm policies were a spectacular success and the seeming intractability of the farm problem merely a manifestation of that success. Farm programs encouraged farmers to improve productivity by mechanizing and purchasing other new inputs. They placed cash in farmers' hands, as well as the access to credit to do so. Acreage allotment programs provided an added incentive to farm active acres more intensively.

Even though the stated goal of farm policies was to restore parity between the farm and non-farm sectors, maintaining crop prices at their unit values, they encouraged farmers to undertake actions that depressed that unit value.[19] Hence, farm programs in practice served to maintain prices above unit values, and even fostered an increasing gap between the two. In doing so, they encouraged the rise of agribusiness seeking to capture farmers' state-supported revenues at taxpayers' expense, creating an ever-more-expensive and entrenched system of entitlements along with a new industry with a vested interest in the continuation of those programs. They increased volatility within the farm sector, contributing to a rapid decline in the number of farms and farmers, and an increase in the average size of farms. In short, farm policy exacerbated and hastened the development of unevenness among farmers. Those that survived the technology treadmill faced a dramatically altered environment with complex and contradictory impacts for the feudal, ancient, and capitalist class structures constituting the family farm hybrid, as well as for the survival strategies of making do and helping out.

The rise of agribusiness

Instead of resulting in falling market prices for corn, technical change with state price supports intensified competition in input markets. Ancient farmers, armed with bulked-up, state-subsidized profits, bumped up against other ancient farmers as they attempted to grow their enterprises and access expanded conditions of existence. This competition among farmers ratcheted up ground rent, increasing the wealth of landowners, and benefiting farmers who innovated and expanded more quickly. Agricultural economists have long argued that the benefits of price support programs mainly accrue to owners of fixed factors of production, especially land, in the form of higher farmland values, while harming younger farmers and renters seeking to expand (Cochrane 1993; Paarlberg and Paarlberg 2000).

In addition to land, the adoption of the new technologies required purchasing inputs previously produced by the farmer himself, including traction power, fodder, feed, seed, and fertilizer. These inputs were now increasingly produced by agribusiness firms, which expanded rapidly in response to government-supported demand from farmers. Hence, competition among ancient farmers coupled with price supports shaped the development and structure of capitalist agribusiness supplying inputs such as machinery, seeds, fertilizer, and other chemicals to farming.

The significance of the cash bonanza enabled by government farm programs was not lost on farm implement companies, for example. Speaking of the CCC loan program, International Harvester Sales Manager, J. L. McCaffrey reported in 1939, "The significance of these corn loans is that they represent 36-cent corn in Minnesota on which 57 cents is obtained by the farmer, with the difference between these two figures representing cash he may use for purchases or other purposes." In other words, farmers would have been getting 36 cents for corn had the CCC loan rate of 57 cents not been in place. Implement companies also noted the benefits of government credit programs to finance farmers' equipment expenditures, thus saving implement dealers the cost and risk of carrying the notes (Clarke 2002, 197). The abundance of revenues in corn farming constituted a veritable feast for agribusinesses, and government programs a perfect recipe for financing their gluttony at taxpayers' expense through the ruse of support for farmers.

Rapidly expanding farm revenues presented opportunities for agribusiness firms to pursue aggressive growth strategies. Since government farm programs helped prop up farmers' demand for purchased inputs, altered demand relative to supply conditions in markets for inputs like tractors and seeds drove a wedge between prices and unit values of these items. As prices diverged from unit values, agribusinesses enjoyed additional revenues, while farmers, as buyers of the more expensive inputs suffered the corresponding negative non-class revenues.

These additional revenues contributed to further developments in the agribusiness firms supplying inputs. What may have been initially a windfall due to demand and supply conditions enabled the pursuit of a deliberate strategy of monopolization. Input suppliers could distribute their additional non-class revenues toward pursuing strategies to maintain the price squeeze on farmers by garnering market power, thereby benefiting from farmers' government payments from price support programs. Such distributions included, for example, distributions for new product development, not only to stay ahead of competitors, but also to keep the hunt for super profits going, thereby intensifying competition among farmers to keep up or catch up with their neighbors; for mergers and acquisitions or other strategies to establish monopoly positions in the industry; or for lobbying and propaganda efforts to maintain and influence government farm policy.

International Harvester, for example, increased expenditures on "engineering and development" by more than 35 percent between 1929 and 1939, in an effort to capture farmers' dollars with new and improved products. The company succeeded in knocking the erstwhile leader, Ford, entirely out of the tractor market by 1928 with its new tricycle-wheeled Farmall. The structure of the industry began moving toward oligopoly during the 1920s, giving implement manufacturers greater power to charge prices above values for access to their products. The number of manufacturers in the industry went from 186 at the peak of the World War I boom in 1921, to roughly 60 by mid-decade. Companies employed a variety of tactics to establish market power. For example, Henry Ford slashed prices for the Fordson in 1922 in an ultimately unsuccessful bid to capture a larger market share. The full-line implement dealers also distributed resources toward pressuring dealers to carry their lines exclusively (*The New York Times* 1938). The eight full-line farm implement manufacturers increased their share of the tractor market from 26 percent in 1921 to 96 percent by 1929. Their share grew to 98.6 percent of the market by 1937, with International Harvester holding over half (Olmstead and Rhode 2001, 684).

These strategies thus appeared to be effective in generating some degree of monopoly power, and thereby maintaining the price squeeze. For farmers, the negative non-class revenue contributed to further changes in farmers' expenditures. These changes took the form of new subsumed class payments to agribusiness firms whenever those firms were able to wield monopoly power such that they could charge a market price for an input that was higher than its unit value. In contrast to the post-World War I slump, when tractor prices declined, the 1929 to 1933 period saw nominal prices little changed, meaning real tractor prices actually rose, then rose more quickly from 1933 to 1935. By 1936, the unreasonably high prices had attracted regulatory attention. Congress charged the FTC with the task of investigating monopoly practices in the implement industry. Among the primary reasons for "agricultural maladjustment" cited in a 1940 USDA report was "growth of monopoly and price fixing by corporations" (USDA 1940a, 5). The report noted that although farmers lacked the organizational capacity to wield market power, agribusiness suffered no such condition. Concentration, consolidation, and growth of capitalist agribusiness continued in the post-World War II period, ultimately producing some of the world's largest corporations.[20]

The competitive struggle among ancient corn farmers therefore became a condition for the continued transfer of subsumed class payments to agribusiness input suppliers. This period saw the beginning of the rise of agribusiness and the process of encroachment of capitalist industry into farming practices. Farm implement companies would be followed by seed, fertilizer, and other chemical companies. Those agribusiness giants had a stake not only in the farm sector but also in the perpetual, technology-induced crisis of that sector and the farm programs enabling it.

Contrary to other accounts (see Lewontin (2008) for example), this process did not result in the increasing role of capitalist class processes in corn-producing family farm enterprises, or in farm production itself, i.e. the "proletarianization" of the farmer." It is true that capitalist agribusiness captured more and more production processes from farmers and, with these, an expanding share of the food dollar. Farmers relied increasingly upon capitalist class processes to carry out farm production in the form of purchased farm inputs. They increasingly specialized in the production of bulk agricultural commodities in order to generate the needed cash for these purchases. Hence, farmers were less insulated, less self-sufficient, and more dependent on the vagaries of markets. In some ways, farmers were also de-skilled, as the specialized knowledge required to manage complex, diversified farming systems was removed from the farm enterprise. Deborah Fitzgerald argues, for example, that in the switch to purchased seeds, farmers' skill at breeding and selecting their own seeds was devalued. The production of such specialized knowledge was transferred to agribusiness firms instead (Fitzgerald 1993). On the other hand, farmers had to acquire new knowledge of different kinds in order to operate the larger, mechanized, specialized, commercial operations. Corlann Gee Bush argues that farmers' jobs became more complex as a result (Bush 1987). In any case, the New Agriculture required farmers to acquire new skills as competent and informed businessmen.

These changes both signaled and necessitated shifts in family farms' survival strategies, to be sure, but they did not signal or necessitate the transformation of the "independent" family farmer into either a capitalist or a capitalist wage laborer. On the contrary, it was this flexibility of the family farm hybrid to adapt and survive at any cost which helped prevent agribusiness firms from taking over farm production. It was more profitable for them to "farm the farmers" rather than to farm the land themselves. Corn Belt family farmers remained a mostly non-capitalist link in an ever-more-extensive chain of production, dominated at either end by capitalist agribusinesses selling them inputs and purchasing their outputs. Capitalist class processes did *not* play an expanded role in farm production itself. In fact, as discussed further below, the same processes of technical change and the ancient hunt for super profits that facilitated the growth of capitalist class processes in agriculture *outside* the farm gate, facilitated the retreat of capitalism *within* it. Ancient class processes in the family farm enterprise were strengthened as a result.

State price supports, however, produced the contradictory situation that threatened their continued existence while simultaneously increasing those with a stake in that existence. As the analysis above suggests, state expenses quickly grew larger as the hunt for super profits continued, continually lowering social unit values and increasing the distance to the unchanged government support price. More and more corn was produced, as well, with the government making up for a growing gap with each and every bushel of corn produced. State expenditures ballooned into entitlements, with constant pressure to expand on one hand, but inviting opposition on the other. Also, as the analysis above suggests, those same government farm programs, when evaluated in terms of their stated objective of resolving the "farm problem," appeared to be an utter failure. Production of supported crops remained high, in spite of government controls over production and marketing, because these could not compensate for improved productivity. Programs encouraged farmers to shift toward production of covered crops – the same crops that were already in surplus. Farm policies transferred non-class revenues to farmers, but were silent about changes in costs (also not surprising given the above analysis) so that production and operating costs continued to rise. The parity ratio averaged only 81 in 1940, compared to 82 in 1930, and 99 in 1920 (Carter et al. 2006; Gardner 2006). Farm programs increased the disparity between farmers, as large scale farmers benefited more than smaller scale ones.

But these were actually signs of success. Farm policies served to reinforce and empower the interests of many of those who were at the table when they were first formulated. They were successful at restarting the technology treadmill after the disastrous crash, and at keeping the hunt for super profits going. In doing so, state policies invited opposition, while also creating the conditions for their continued existence by increasing those not only with a stake in their existence, but also the resources to shape political outcomes accordingly. Initially, market prices remained high through World War II and beyond, bolstered by continued U.S. aid abroad as well as Cold War military rearmament (Jellison 1993). These conditions enabled the expansion of commodity programs to a total of 166 commodities, as price supports were inexpensive to maintain. Beginning in 1953 with the end of the Korean War, prices began a secular decline, driven in part by rapid productivity growth. As government stocks and CCC outlays increased, political pressure mounted to alter program provisions or to end them altogether. Attempts to reduce supply and increase demand through export subsidies, land set-aside programs, food aid, and nutritional programs were not enough to offset the impacts of the technology treadmill (Paarlberg and Paarlberg 2000). Parity measures themselves became the object of continual struggle, only to be eventually abandoned and price support levels continually ratcheted downward.[21] Differently positioned farmers were impacted differently by these developments, and responded accordingly. For many, that meant staying on the technology treadmill created by the constantly changing flows of surplus back and forth as the scramble for super profits continued.

The combination of state price supports and production controls at first served as a floor under the price of important agricultural commodities, and thereby under the price of food as well. These measures thus constrained the rate of exploitation in industry from being higher than it might otherwise have been had food prices been allowed to fall to reflect their unit values. This point was not lost on agribusiness or other industry and, as soon as these measures were put into place, various interests went to work to alter program provisions by dismantling them. As early as 1949, Secretary of Agriculture Charles F. Brannan recommended replacing price-supporting loan rates with direct payments to farmers. As competition in world grain markets intensified after World War II, grain exporters were successful in winning a reduction in loan rates compensated with direct payments starting in 1962 (Paarlberg and Paarlberg 2000). The operation of these measures was gradually shifted along these lines across the decades, eroding the mechanisms supporting prices paid by those purchasing commodities from farmers. Today, farmers continue to receive revenues based on the state-supported fair market value of their crops, called the "loan rate," but there is no floor under the market price of corn which agribusinesses and other buyers pay because the government no longer purchases and stores it, it merely makes up the difference between the market price and the loan rate whenever the crop is sold. All employers reap the benefits of improved agricultural productivity through cheapened wage goods, allowing a rising rate of class exploitation in industry while supporting the real wage. Agribusinesses continue to benefit from the state-supported competition among ancient farmers.

Surviving the treadmill: making do, helping out, and the family farm hybrid

As technical change shaped competition among farm enterprises, it altered the distribution of costs and benefits from technical change among and within them. Different farm enterprises were differently positioned to adopt new technologies and to benefit from that process. The survival strategies of making do and helping out were impacted accordingly. Different class structures within the family farm were differently impacted by these processes as well. I argue that the ancient and feudal class processes were probably strengthened by these developments in many ways. As previously discussed, capitalist class processes actually retreated from Corn Belt family farms, even as they grew in importance in the larger food and agriculture system. Thus, the industrialization of farming did not entail its transition to capitalism, but actually the strengthening of its non-capitalist class structures.

The workings of the technology treadmill continued in the post-war era, exacerbating differences and contributing to an increasing unevenness among farmers. As already noted, prosperous farmers were already well-positioned to adopt new technologies more quickly and, using their super profits, to gobble up the assets of their neighbors and to grow even larger. In addition, the larger farmers who could purchase tractors first enabled them to use less hired help, thus reducing income earning opportunities for medium and small-size farmers and their children (Neth 1998, 227). Many small farms could not keep up with the rising cash production costs that accompanied the shifts in farming practices. About 10 percent of Midwestern farms failed in the first five years after the war (Jellison 1993). Although fewer in number, the Midwestern farms that survived the technology treadmill emerged from World War II and its aftermath larger and more prosperous, with more modern equipment in both farm enterprise and farm household than their predecessors (Jellison 1993). According to the Census of Agriculture, the percentage of Midwestern farms owning in 1945 tractors ranged from 27.8 in Missouri to 81.4 in North Dakota. By 1950, the percentages were 43.6 and 89.2, respectively (Jellison 1993).

As the labor requirements of corn farming declined with mechanization, shifting the conditions of hybrid farm production, ancient class processes were probably strengthened on both larger and smaller surviving farms. Mechanization transformed labor processes, reducing the time and physical effort required to complete necessary tasks. Among the reasons farmers cited for adopting a tractor, according to a 1942 USDA study by two Bureau of Agricultural

Economics (BAE) sociologists, were that 'it saves time,' 'it eliminates some of the harder work,' and 'it makes possible a better job of farming" (Jellison 1993, 109). The purchase of the tractor was also found to be motivated by the desire to "keep sons on the farm" by improving the conditions and interest of farm work, hence strengthening the attachment of the ancient farmer's serf-apprentices (USDA 1940b). Ancient class processes benefited as more work on more land could be done by a lone producer, without the aid of other workers and in less time. In addition, ancient farmers of completely horseless farms enjoyed increased autonomy as they were no longer at the beck and call of their live-stocks' needs. Farm animals required daily and continual care. Tractors did not. Hence, mechanization increased the ancient farmer's discretion over his own time. One farm wife was quoted in a 1936 Caterpillar tractor pamphlet explaining,

> Now when a picnic comes along my husband can't say, "Oh, the feed is about gone." ... Or if the family wants to go to the Lake for a few days, we don't need to worry about the tractor getting into somebody's field of wheat, or doing without a drink.
>
> (Bush 1987, 221)

On larger farms the income generated was sufficient so that the ancient farmer did not have to seek employment off the farm, and the expanded access to new machinery and productivity-enhancing technologies continued to strengthen these ancient class processes. On smaller farms, those that were "long on labor and short on land," mechanization may have meant that the ancient farmer's time or physical capacity to work, or both, were freed from the production of field crops, and could be allocated to other farm production activities to increase total farm income. Another common outcome as cash requirements increased was to devote less time to ancient farm production, freeing the farmer for work off the farm earning income to supplement the ancient farm enterprise (Hurt 2003). One or both of these strategies may help explain the results of one 1933 Wisconsin time use study that seemed to show "more work for father." Farm men with tractors were found to work longer days on average than those without tractors (Kline 1997, 379; Neth 1998, 227). This could have been related to the addition of off-farm employment for farm men, or to the fact that the reduced physical toil of farming allowed ancient farmers to spend longer hours doing it.

The labor saved by the purchase of a tractor would have included not only that of the farmer himself, but also of his family and hired laborers. Figure 2.7 shows how the decline in farm employment of both unpaid family laborers and hired hands coincided with farm mechanization, beginning during the 1930s, and then accelerating after World War II. The relative impacts on family laborers and hired laborers differed across farms. For some, mechanization meant that males replaced not only hired workers, but also wives and children in field work. For others, mechanization merely meant that field work was shifted from hired hands to wives and children who took on a greater role (Jellison 1993). This indicates that while feudal class processes may have either retreated from or expanded in the family farm enterprise, to the extent that hired laborers indicated the presence of capitalist class processes, these largely retreated as a result of mechanization.

One reason was that the tractor replaced non-purchased C-goods with purchased C-goods. Farm horses could be purchased, but were more often reproduced on the farm, as were the oats, corn and hay that were their feed. Tractors and fuel had to be purchased from off-farm manufacturers, but saved on the labor required in caring for horses and raising oats and hay. Raising an acre of oats required between six and eight hours per acre. The time spent haying depended on the number of cuttings per season, but Ankli estimated roughly nine hours per acre for two cuttings (Ankli 1980, 142). (Clarke estimates 6.4 hours per acre for hay (Clarke 2002, 275).) Thus, several hours of labor would have been saved by the replacement of each horse. Of course, part of this savings was offset since farmers spent extra time in repair and maintenance of tractors as well.

The shift from horses to tractors had a dramatic impact on the need for hired labor during harvest. For example, Midwestern farmers who grew grains such as wheat required a horse-powered combine during harvest. Prior to mechanization, each combine required up to 44 horses to pull it, as well as up to nine men to operate it. A large operation might have used four or five such combines and their crews to complete the grain harvest. With the purchase of a tractor to pull the combine, none of the horses and only a fraction or even none of the hired hands was needed (Bush 1987).

The feudal class processes of the family farm household and enterprise also interacted with the hunt for super profits among ancients in contradictory ways. The farm wife's subsidies of unpaid labor, for example, could hinder the initial purchase of new technologies, but serve to finance them after adoption. There is ample evidence of the importance of making do in allowing cash-poor and smaller farmers to delay the purchase of a tractor. Implement manufacturers and government agents were constantly frustrated by farmers' unwillingness to assign market prices (or any prices at all) to family labor, because doing so made the purchase of a tractor much less attractive. Clarke found that a significant proportion of farmers who met the acreage threshold for tractors in the 1920s, nevertheless did not purchase one because they did not value family labor at market prices (Clarke 2002). Translated into class terms, feudal farm wives were subsidizing ancient farmers' consumption through practices of making do.

If he did seek to enter the fray with his innovating neighbors, the ancient farmer's actions had contradictory consequences for the family farm's other class structures, as well as farm family members, and necessitated shifts in the strategies of making do and helping out. The needs of the farm enterprise continued to supersede those of the farm household, so that for less prosperous farms, the purchase of a tractor meant forgoing modern household conveniences. In a 1946 letter to *Wallace's Farmer*, a Nebraska farm wife explained,

When Dad got the new manure scoop, the elevator and other modern farm tools, daughter and I approved, feeling that one of these days it would be our turn to enjoy electricity and a few modern conveniences. Just when we thought we had him convinced, what does he do? Orders another new tractor for the boys!

(Jellison 1993)

At the same time, the purchase of a tractor lightened the burden of farm women's and children's work in significant ways, thereby strengthening the feudal, as well as the ancient class structure of the family farm. The 1936 Caterpillar tractor pamphlet with the slogan, "At last we wives can have vacations" was directed at farm women for just this reason (Bush 1987; Garkovich and Bokemeier 1988, 211). Helping out in field work became less strenuous with mechanization, as did some of a farm wife's household work. For example, a tractor could be used for pumping water for the kitchen or gardens when not in use in the fields (Jellison 1993). A 1940 *New York Times* article on "Machines on the Farm" noted that since the majority of family farms relied very little on hired labor, "the main result of mechanization on the farm is not to lay off workers but to shorten the working hours of the farm family and to relieve it of much drudgery" (*The New York Times* 1940b). Even if they did not rely primarily on hired labor, many farms did so for short bursts during busy times of the year, and the purchase of a tractor relieved the farm wife's burden of planning, cooking, and cleaning for hired hands.

In addition, as farm enterprises mechanized and specialized, women's farm and home production activities in the barnyard and garden declined. Egg, poultry, vegetable, and milk production, for example, relocated to specialized commercial operations concentrated in particular geographical regions rather than being dispersed on farms throughout the country. According to the Census of Agriculture, for example, in 1900, 98 percent (5.6 million) of 5.7 million farms had chickens. By 1950, the proportion had fallen to 78 percent (4.2 million) of 5.4 million farms. The 1950s and 1960s saw an acceleration in specialization, so that by 1969, only 17 percent of the 2.7 million farms counted in the census kept chickens (Gardner 2006). Electricity, home freezers and other labor-saving appliances, along with better roads, automobiles, and greater access to store-bought items meant that women spent less time butchering, canning, and processing meat and produce. As Corlann Gee Bush argues, "the 1920s to 1960s [were] the decades when the market economy completed its 'hostile takeover' of women's domestic production – forcing women, particularly farm women, out of 'business'" (Bush 1987, 223).

This decline was reinforced by government farm programs that provided support for ancient class processes in the family farm enterprise in livestock and crop production, but not for farm women's feudal class processes in the family farm enterprise in poultry, dairy, fruit, and vegetable production. The gender and class bias of New Deal farm programs toward supporting ancient class processes on middle and upper class farms meant that they failed to support these activities which were such a significant component of farm families' standards of living before and during the Great Depression, in spite of farm women's efforts to get these concerns addressed (Jellison 1993). The USDA instead continued to push the agenda of farm enterprise and farm home modernization in order to achieve the domestic ideal in the countryside. The post-war era saw a renewed and intensified campaign to define farm women's place as in the home, not outside or in the fields. In the March 1947 issue of *Successful Farming*, for example, one reader wrote, "No, I don't think a woman's place is outdoors! There's enough to do inside" (Carpenter 2000). For many observers, farm women's "freedom" from their traditional farm production activities meant that they could at long last concentrate exclusively on their role as homemakers. The decline in farm women's distinctive production activities seemed to signal their growing similarity to urban women in terms of lives, living conditions, and identity (Jellison 1993).

These changes seem to indicate a retreat of feudal class processes from the family farm enterprise in favor of the family farm household and, indeed, this may have been the case for some farm women, particularly those of wealthier farmers. Some historians identify the decline in farm women's production activities with a loss in status as co-producers in the farm-enterprise, and hence a strengthening of patriarchal, feudal class structures in the farm household (Bush 1987). However, the intensified homemaker rhetoric notwithstanding, farm women's activities in helping out and making do remained crucial to the survival of the family farm enterprise. These activities merely shifted form. As Katherine Jellison explains, "In the postwar era, the tractor and the off-farm job merely replaced the poultry house and the garden as symbols of women's work beyond the home" (Jellison 1993, 179). Again, the impacts of tractors differed according to income. As some farmers grew ever wealthier and more productive, and able to purchase the "domestic ideal" for their wives, large numbers of smaller farmers nevertheless hung on (and still do) by exploiting a different strategy – supplementing farm receipts with their wives' labor and transfers to the farm enterprise and household through the altered strategies of making do and helping out.

In fact, many farm women's participation in field work increased, becoming less contingent and more regular as mechanization reduced the physical strain of this work (and labor-saving home appliances and the decline of their other farm production activities freed their time to do so). According to a 1960 article in *Wallace's Farmer*,

> [T]oday's farm women are doing more outside work than ever before. Many put in long hours in the fields on a tractor or other machinery throughout the growing season. Wives, plus machinery, have taken the place of hired men or other outside help.
>
> (Murphy 1960; Jellison 1993; Carpenter 2000)

A *Wallace's Farmer* poll of Iowa farm women discussed in the article, found that 49 percent helped their husbands with field work (Murphy 1960). In addition to helping out directly in the farm fields, farm women increasingly did other chores like driving grain trucks, going to town for machinery parts, and keeping farm books.

In addition to these changes in farm women's role in helping out in the farm enterprise, increased cash expenses associated with mechanized farming led them to alter strategies of making do as well. During the 1950s, agricultural publications began noting the new phenomenon of farm women working in town, as farm wives increasingly took off-farm employment to make ends meet (Jellison 1993; Hurt 2003). A 1956 article in *Wallace's Farmer* on the increasing prevalence (25 percent) of "farm home-makers" of all ages among female wage earners in Wayne County, Iowa, proclaimed that "Mrs. Farmer has turned career girl." Farm women worked in a variety of occupations, including as secretaries, teachers, retail and filing clerks, waitresses, bookkeepers, and nurses. As their feudal production activities in the family farm enterprise and household declined, farm women's extra time could be spent in employment elsewhere and their wages earned in enterprises off the farm shifted to purchase consumption items for farm family members and to subsidize the cash requirements of the ancient farm enterprise. One Wayne County farm woman noted that her salary would be used for "school clothing, groceries, tractor fuel and farm payments." As the author of the article concluded, "Mom has come to town so dad and the kids can stay on the farm" (Clayton 1956). Farm women's feudal subsidies to other family members may have changed form as a result of farm mechanization, but the strategies of helping out and making do to subsidize the family farm's survival remained.

These shifts in the strategies of helping out and making do need not have entailed the disappearance of feudal structures from the family farm enterprise or household. While some farm women were undoubtedly able to utilize their changed roles in the farm enterprise and in off-farm work to challenge the patriarchal authority of their husbands, thereby weakening feudal class structures in family farms, countervailing forces served to strengthen them as well. As Zoe Murphy, the editor of the "Homemaking Today" section of *Wallace's Farmer* observed, "Women who work away from home, whether it's a job in town or helping out-of-doors, really have two jobs. They carry responsibility for both the care of the children and up-keep of the home" (Murphy 1960). In other words, farm women's feudal serfdom in the family farm household remained intact. The rhetoric of housewifery and homemaking disguised women's work outside the home, enabling while also devaluing it. Women's field work was still described as "helping out." In addition to driving tractors or other machinery in the fields, helping out in the farm enterprise entailed many tasks that could be tacked onto a farm wife's home production activities. Going to town to shop for groceries, for example, could be combined with picking up spare parts for farm machinery or dropping them off for repair. To the extent that farm women's farm chores were viewed as part of their regular household tasks, they were less visible and hence less valued (Bush 1987). In addition, farm women sometimes had less discretion over their own time with new forms of field work. While their work in the barnyard and garden had been largely unsupervised, in the field they were under the direct supervision of their husbands. Even a farm woman's off-farm work was enabled by her husband's identity as the farmer engaged in agricultural work (and hers as "merely" his wife), leaving her "free" to leave the farm to seek employment. If such work in the field or off-farm reduced farm women's isolation and drudgery, they may have been content to continue in their positions as feudal household serfs, particularly if farm mechanization and the increased cash income enabled the adoption of labor-saving household technologies as well. In that case, farm women would even have experienced and tolerated an increased rate of feudal exploitation in the family farm household along with their field work or off-farm employment. None of the farm women in Wayne County, for example, professed to have any plans to return to the farm full-time. The author noted that the women were willing to tolerate the "dual role," not only for the extra money, but also because "they get a kick out of it" (Clayton 1956).

Conclusion

Nearly five million farms ceased to exist between 1935 and 2012. The 1950s and 1960s were decades of particularly rapid change. Mary Conger's vivid description of how she and her husband struggled to keep their large Kansas dairy farm afloat is probably the most famous statement of the technology treadmill as seen through the eyes of a farmer's wife in the midst of it all:

> When that first slash in farm prices came six years ago, we doubled our milking herd in an effort to increase gross income so that, in turn, we could meet our fixed charges – such as interest and taxes – and the rising cost of things we must buy. We built a new labor-saving milking parlor – a sort of assembly-ling milking system. But then came years when our crops were cut by drought, hail and wet weather, and we fell behind on the feed bill for the cattle. In good years, we struggled to catch up. We tripled the milking herd. Milk prices declined further. Costs went on up. We were on a treadmill, always running faster just to keep in the same place.
>
> (Conger 1960)

Even though their farm's gross income placed it in the upper 3 percent of farms in the U.S., and it was "adequately capitalized and highly mechanized for large-volume production," the Conger's were "caught in a merciless cost-price squeeze, and each year that economic turnbuckle tightens another notch" (Conger 1960). Her story became a rallying point for struggling farmers after her article was first published in the *Saturday Evening Post*, and then read into the *Congressional Record.* It illustrates how competition and technical change yielded a poison fruit of falling prices for output, rising prices for inputs, and mounting debt, even for "successful" farmers, as they sought to "modernize" and expand.

Farm programs intensified technical change in farm production begun with the arrival of the farm tractor in the 1920s. In doing so, state intervention – ostensibly on behalf of an idealized family farm – gutted that same institution as it gave farmers the means of cannibalizing each other in a vicious competitive process. Farm programs encouraged the overproduction of particular food crops – bulk commodities that form the raw material in an extensive chain of production used to create and redistribute value from small to larger farmers and agribusiness intermediaries. They encouraged the rise of capitalist agribusiness at taxpayers' expense, situating farmers as conduits for cash payments from the government. They created an ever-more-expensive and entrenched system of entitlements for farmers, along with a far-flung configuration of industries with a vested interest in the continuation of those programs. They increased volatility, crisis, and disparity within the farm sector, hollowing out the "middle class" of farmers, and leaving few very large, and many very small farms facing different economic circumstances and succeeding in different ways. Today, the largest farms account for the majority of production, while the smallest account for the majority of farms. In 2010, for example, according to USDA typology, the largest farms (family farms with sales over $250,000 per year and non-family farms) account for the majority of the value of production (84 percent), while the smallest, which farm only part-time and rely on off-farm incomes, account for the majority of farms (88 percent). Million-dollar farms make up about 2 percent of all farms, but account for 53 percent of the value of production (Hoppe and Banker 2010).

Structural changes in agriculture served to strengthen the non-capitalist class structures in the family farms that survived, both small and large. In this way, the family farm hybrid suffered ongoing crisis while also remaining an enduring organizational form. This resilience was a result of that complex hybrid class structure which furnished both the vulnerability, as well as the flexibility to respond to crisis through the altered strategies of making do and helping out. As some farmers grew ever wealthier and more productive, large numbers of smaller farmers nevertheless hung on through these adaptations. In 1930, only one third of farmers worked off-farm for a significant period of time during the year (defined by the USDA as over 100 days). In 2005, over 90 percent of farm households had off-farm income (Dimitri et al. 2005). Most farm households derived most of their income from off-farm sources. While the mean farm operator household income in 2007 was $88,900 (median was $54,000), only about 13 percent of this income ($11,733) came from farming. Since three of the four categories of small farms in the USDA typology have negative farm earnings on average, their non-farm earnings are more than 100 percent of their household income (Hoppe and Banker 2010). They are, in effect, paying for the "independence" of farming through subsidies from off-farm income of all sorts.

Non-capitalist family farmers have subsidized others in the economy as well. The contradictory trajectory of technical change and agricultural industrialization helped secure the conditions for successful industrial capitalist development in the broader economy, including cheap and abundant food and a newly "freed" mass of landless laborers. Today, families in the U.S. spend a historically low share of disposable income on food – 9.8 percent in 2011 compared to 24.2 percent in 1930. (Clauson 2013). Cheaper food means that workers' real wages may rise even as the value of labor power declines. This situation enables a rising rate of exploitation of workers, who nevertheless have access to (and thus provide a market for) additional goods and services. As Resnick and Wolff (2006) have argued, this combination enabled the long post-war capitalist expansion in the United States, and cheap food, enabled by the technology treadmill, played no small part. In addition, millions of workers were "released" from farming, and available to work in the growing capitalist industries. In 1930, 21.5 percent of the work force was employed on farms. Today, less than 2 percent of the population lives on or is employed by farms (Dimitri, et al. 2005). Thus the crisis and dislocation associated with the state-sponsored technology treadmill in farming were crucial in fueling capitalist growth in the broader post-war U.S. economy. Those family farms that survived ranked among the most productive agricultural institutions in human history, but the price of that achievement was the continued exploitation of farm women, children, and men. As Mary Conger observed in 1960, "The most gigantic subsidy in the United States is not the Federal agricultural price-support program, but the unpaid or underpaid labor that farmers and their families contribute to the production of cheap food for the American people" (Conger 1960).

Notes

1 Commercial fertilizers include organic nitrates and inorganic manufactured nitrates. The cost of producing the latter declined dramatically beginning in the 1940s so that the increased use of inorganic, sometimes called chemical, fertilizers accounts for most of the dramatic increase in usage especially after World War II (Gardner 2002, 22–23).
2 Net farm income is the value of farm output minus expenditures on inputs, not including the cost of depreciation (Gardner 2006).
3 For the details regarding the development and adoption of hybrid corn, see Appendix B.
4 King cites the Census as indicating the number of horses and mules on farms peaked in 1920, with the number of horses and mules in cities peaking earlier, sometime between 1910 and 1920 (King 1929).
5 In their study of the controversy in the interwar period, Olmstead and Rhode point out how the rhetoric of opposing sides in this technology debate continues to echo in debates about farm technology today. One example is the debate over genetically modified crops or GMOs. Now, as then, the notion of inevitability along with charges of the backwardness of opponents is a rhetorical tool employed by the pro-GMO side of the debate (Olmstead and Rhode 1994).
6 The following equation signifies the ancient class structure with super profits:

Ancient Class Structure with Super profits: $S(A)^{FFE} + NCR_{SP} > SSCP(A)^{FFE}$

The left hand side signifies ancient surplus produced in the family farm enterprise with the addition of the non-class revenue of super profit. The term on the right hand side signifies ancient subsumed class payments.
7 I assume unless otherwise specified that the market price of corn is equal to its value.

8 The following equation gives the expression for super profits:

$$NCR_{SP} = \left(\left(\frac{W}{UV} \right) - \left(\frac{W}{UV} \right)_{PR} \right) \times UV$$

Where NCR_{SP} stands for the non-class revenue of super profit, W for exchange value, and UV for use value; and the subscript PR stands for private.

9 This trend would reverse notably during the Great Depression, when tractor prices actually rose in real terms (Olmstead and Rhode 2001).

10 Small improvements could make a tremendous difference. For example, the invention of an adequate air cleaner significantly extended the life of the tractor. Otherwise, the dust and particles stirred up from plowing and other field operations could get sucked into the tractor's engine, causing it to seize (Martini 2003).

11 The parity ratio reported here is the ratio of the index of prices received by farmers to the index of prices paid to farmers, with 1909–1914 = 100. The parity ratio was originally intended as a measure of the standard of living of farm people. Prices paid include various production expenses plus interest, taxes, and wages, as well as living expenses (Gardner 2006).

12 The Wallace family of Iowa produced three generations of prominent national agricultural leaders, all named Henry. Henry A.'s grandfather served as the head of the Country Life Commission and founded the national weekly *Wallace's Farmer.* Henry A.'s father, Henry C. Wallace edited the paper until Warren G. Harding appointed him Secretary of Agriculture in 1921 in the midst of the post-war farm depression. Henry A. took over the editorship of the paper at that time. He later served as Secretary of Agriculture, then Vice President under FDR. He narrowly lost the nomination for vice president to Harry Truman in 1944, and ran as the Progressive Party presidential candidate in 1948 (Meller 2005).

13 Government farm programs explicitly or implicitly ignored feudal forms of farm production, including sharecropping, as well as farm women's feudal farm production in Midwestern family farms.

14 These payments constituted a new source of non-class revenue from the state as follows:

$$NCR_R = P_{FMV} \times \overline{\overline{UV}}_{BP} \times N$$

Farmers' revenues from rental payments from the state were equal to the government-set price at the "fair market value" for the crop (P_{FMV}), based on the goal of 1909–1914 parity, times the average number of bushels the crop yielded during the base period (for corn it was initially 1928 to 1932) ($\overline{U}\,\overline{V}_{BP}$), times the number of acres (or portions of those acres) enrolled in the allotment program (N).

15 These trends were particularly evident in the cotton South, as landlords evicted their tenants, consolidated plots, and mechanized causing massive dislocations and radically changed Southern agriculture.

16 The new revenue position for price support payments (NCR_{PS}) can be expressed as follows:

$$NCR_{PS} = \left| P_{FMV} - P_M \right| \times UV$$

$P_{FMV} - P_M$ is the difference between the government-set price and the market price, and UV is the number of bushels, or use values.

17 The situation for innovators can be expressed as follows:

$$P_{FMV} > (W/UV) > (W/UV)_{PR}$$

For non-innovators:

$$P_{FMV} = (W/UV)_{PR} > (W/UV)$$

The new revenue position can be expressed in equation form as follows:

$$NCR_{FMV} = \left(P_{FMV} - \left(\frac{W}{UV} \right) \right) \times UV$$

18 The total change in revenues for all farmers was therefore as follows:

$$\Delta Revenus = NCR_{SP} + NCR_{FMV}$$

19 "Parity means a price for the farmer's product which will give it an exchange value for things the farmer needs to buy equivalent to that in a specified base period. The base period used as a par is the five prewar years 1909–14." The index of current prices paid by farmers included prices paid for the "necessaries of life as well as for items used up in production," as well as taxes on real estate and interest charges. In Marxian terms, then, parity could be considered a rough approximation to C+V plus a portion of S (at least that portion of S distributed for subsumed class payments for taxes and interest payments). Farm labor costs in terms of wages were not included in the price index used to calculate parity (*Time* 1946).
20 Cargill, for example, was the world's largest private corporation in 2013, according to Forbes.com.
21 For example, the farm bloc tangled regularly with other lawmakers over adjustments to the parity formula, including altering the base years, adding interest and taxes into the index of prices paid (which was done starting in 1935), and adding farm wages (*Time* 1946).

References

Ankli, Robert E. 1980. "Horses Vs. Tractors on the Corn Belt." *Agricultural History* 54 (1) (January 1): 134–148.
Ball, E., S. L. Wang, and R. Nehring. 2012. "Agricultural Productivity in the U.S." USDA Economic Research Service. July 5. Available online at www.ers.usda.gov/data-products/agricultural-productivity-in-the-us/documentation-and-methods.aspx#. UgqumW0yGSo.
Bush, Corlann Gee. 1987. " 'He Isn't Half So Cranky as He Used to Be': Agricultural Mechanization, Comparable Worth, and the Changing Farm Family." In *"To Toil the Livelong Day" America's Woman at Work, 1780–1980,* by Carol Groneman, 213–229. Ithaca: Cornell University Press.
Carpenter, Stephanie A. 2000. " 'Women Who Work in the Field': The Changing Role of Farm and Nonfarm Women on the Farm." *Agricultural History* 74 (2) (April 1): 465–474.
Carter, Susan B., Scott Sigmund Gartner, Michael R. Haines, Alan L. Olmstead, Richard Sutch, and Gavin Wright, eds. 2006. *Historical Statistics of the United States, Earliest Times to the Present: Millennial Edition Online.* New York: Cambridge University Press. Available online at http://hsus.cambridge.org/HSUSWeb/HSUSEntryServlet.
Casey, Janet Galligani. 2004. " 'This Is Your Magazine': Domesticity, Agrarianism, and *The Farmer's Wife.*" *American Periodicals: A Journal of History, Criticism, and Bibliography* 14(2): 179–211.
Clarke, Sally H. 2002. *Regulation and the Revolution in United States Farm Productivity.* New York: Cambridge University Press.
Clauson, Annette. 2013. "Food Expenditures." USDA Economic Research Service. August 16. Available online at www.ers.usda.gov/data-products/food-expenditures. aspx#.UiJZyD8yHTo.

Clayton, John. 1956. "Farm Wife Turns Wage Earner." *Wallace's Farmer*, October 20.

Cochrane, Willard Wesley. 1993. *The Development of American Agriculture: a Historical Analysis*. Minneapolis: University of Minnesota Press.

Conger, Mary. 1960. "The Farmer's Side of the Case." *Saturday Evening Post* 232 (41) (April 9): 36–102.

Daily Boston Globe. 1936. "Wallace Attacks G.O.P. Farm Stand." August 12.

Dimitri, Carolyn, Anne Effland, and Neilson Conklin. 2005. "The 20th Century Transformation of U.S. Agriculture and Farm Policy." Economic Information Bulletin 3. Washington, DC: USDA Economic Research Service. Available online at www.ers.usda.gov/publications/eib-economic-information-bulletin/eib3.aspx#.UiJP_T8yHTo.

Fitzgerald, Deborah. 1993. "Farmers Deskilled: Hybrid Corn and Farmers' Work." *Technology and Culture* 34 (2) (April): 324–343. doi:10.2307/3106539.

Fitzgerald, Deborah. 2003. *Every Farm a Factory: The Industrial Ideal in American Agriculture*. New Haven: Yale University Press.

Gardner, Bruce L. 2006. *American Agriculture in the Twentieth Century: How It Flourished and What It Cost*. Cambridge: Harvard University Press.

Garkovich, Lorraine, and Janet Bokemeier. 1988. "Agricultural Mechanization and American Farm Women's Economic Roles." In *Women and Farming*, edited by Wava Haney and Jane Knowles, 211–228. Rural Studies. Boulder and London: Westview Press.

Hoppe, Robert A., and Banker, David E. 2010. "Structure and Finances of U.S. Farms: Family Farm Report, 2010 Edition." USDA Economic Research Service. Available online at www.ers.usda.gov/Publications/EIB24/.

Hurt, Douglas R. 2003. *Problems of Plenty: The American Farmer in the Twentieth Century*. Chicago: Ivan R Dee.

The Des Moines Register. 1933. "Iowan Gets First U.S. Corn Loan." November 25.

Jellison, Katherine. 1993. *Entitled to Power*. Chapel Hill: University of North Carolina Press.

King, Willford I. 1929. "The Gasoline Engine and the Farmer's Income." *Journal of Farm Economics* 11 (1) (January 1): 64–73. doi:10.2307/1230495.

Kline, Ronald R. 1997. "Ideology and Social Surveys: Reinterpreting the Effects of 'Laborsaving' Technology on American Farm Women." *Technology and Culture* 38 (2) (April 1): 355–385.

Lighthall, D. R, and R. S. Roberts. 1995. "Towards an Alternative Logic of Technological Change: Insights from Corn Belt Agriculture." *Journal of Rural Studies* 11 (3) (July).

Lewontin, R. C. 2008. "The Maturing of Capitalist Agriculture: Farmer as Proletarian." In *Hungry for Profit: The Agribusiness Threat to Farmers, Food, and the Environment*, edited by Fred Magdoff, John Bellamy Foster, and Frederick H. Buttel, 93–106. New York: Monthly Review Press.

Macy, Loring K. 1938. *Changes in Technology and Labor Requirements in Crop Production: Corn*. Works Progress Administration. Washington, DC: Government Printing Office.

Martini, Dinah Duffy. 2003. "Technological Change in US Agriculture: The Case of Substitution of Gasoline Tractor Power for Horse Power." PhD Dissertation. University of Washington.

Marx, Karl. 1975. *Capital: A Critique of Political Economy*. Vol. 1. New York: International Publishers.

Meller, Marcia. 2005. "The Wallace Family – An Iowa Agricultural Dynasty." Iowa

Pathways: Iowa History Resources for Students and Teachers. Available online at www.iptv.org/iowapathways/mypath.cfm?ounid=ob_000343.

Murphy, Zoe. 1960. "Women Who Work in the Field." *Wallace's Farmer*, December 3.

Neth, Mary C. 1998. *Preserving the Family Farm: Women, Community, and the Foundations of Agribusiness in the Midwest, 1900–1940*. Baltimore: The Johns Hopkins University Press.

Olmstead, Alan L., and Paul W. Rhode. 1994. "The Agricultural Mechanization Controversy of the Interwar Years." *Agricultural History* 68 (3) (July 1): 35–53.

Olmstead, Alan L., and Paul W. Rhode. 2001. "Reshaping the Landscape: The Impact and Diffusion of the Tractor in American Agriculture, 1910–1960." *The Journal of Economic History* 61 (3): 663–698.

Paarlberg, R., and D. Paarlberg. 2000. "Agricultural Policy in the Twentieth Century." *Agricultural History* 74 (2): 136–161.

Resnick, Stephen A. 2006. "Class, Contradiction and the Capitalist Economy." In *New Departures in Marxian Theory*, by Stephen A. Resnick and Richard D. Wolff, 238–252. London and New York: Routledge.

Resnick, Stephen A., and Richard D. Wolff. 2006. "Exploitation, Consumption, and the Uniqueness of U.S. Capitalism." In *New Departures in Marxian Theory*, by Stephen A. Resnick and Richard D. Wolff, 341–353. London and New York: Routledge.

Reynoldson, L. A. 1922. "Shall I Buy a Tractor?: (for a Corn-belt Farm)." USDA Farmers' Bulletin 1299. Washington, DC: Government Printing Office.

The New York Times. 1926. "Farmers to Stress Relief." December 5.

The New York Times. 1937. "Man with the Hoe Losing to Tractor." July 18.

The New York Times. 1938. "Farm Tool Makers Assailed by FTC." June 7.

The New York Times. 1940a. "McCormick Calls Machines A Benefit." April 25.

The New York Times. 1940b. "Machines on the Farm." April 28.

Time. 1946. "AGRICULTURE: Faith, Hope, & Parity." April 15. Available online at www.time.com/time/magazine/article/0,9171,886957,00.html.

Time. 1959. "Agriculture: The Pushbutton Cornucopia." March 19. Available online at www. time.com/time/magazine/article/0,9171,825703,00.html.

United States Department of Agriculture (USDA). 1915. "Social and Labor Needs of Farm Women." 103. Washington, DC: Government Printing Office.

United States Department of Agriculture (USDA). 1940a. *Achieving a Balanced Agriculture*. USDA.

United States Department of Agriculture (USDA). 1940b. *Technology on the Farm, a Special Report by an Interbureau Committee and the Bureau of Agricultural Economics of the United States Department of Agriculture*. Washington, DC: Government Printing Office.

Wallace, Henry A. 1932. "A Declaration of Interdependence." New Deal Network. Available online at http://newdeal.feri.org/wallace/haw05.htm.

Wallace, Henry A. 1937. *Technology, Corporations, and the General Welfare*. Chapel Hill: University of North Carolina Press.

4   Conclusion

In this book, I present a contradictory class history of U.S. agriculture using the example of Midwestern corn-producing family farms in the early twentieth century. No one else has examined the family farm in this way. In developing and applying an overdeterminist, Marxian class analysis to an area previously unexamined by others in this tradition, this book represents a contribution toward extending that literature.

In doing so, I bring new insights into the broader Marxian literature on agriculture, class structural transformation and the "Agrarian Question." A common interpretation of Marx's theory of history is that it is teleological and universal, a prescribed path of development that holds across time and space. In this perspective, feudal and ancient forms of the class process necessarily precede, and must inevitably give way to capitalist class processes. Reflecting this view is the language of transition, or "the laws of motion of capitalist development," which identifies feudal and ancient class structures as "pre-capitalist" or "transitional" modes of production. For example, although Maurice Dobb and Paul Sweezy advance different positions in the debate over the transition from feudalism to capitalism, both share the concept that the ancient, which they call the "pre-capitalist petty mode of production" and "pre-capitalist commodity production," respectively, emerged from the feudal mode of production and presaged the growth of capitalism in Western Europe. (Resnick and Wolff 1979; Gabriel 1990; Sweezy et al. 1992). Each form of the class process marches across history in a predetermined order, essential but transitional precursors to the emergence of capitalism. Capitalist development, therefore, is inevitably accompanied by the elimination of "pre-capitalist" forms.

Applying this interpretation of Marx to agriculture generates a conundrum: How can we explain the persistence of non-capitalist forms, such as family farms, within developed capitalist economies? Hence, the "agrarian question" has continually provoked Marxian scholarship and debate across disciplines and time periods. Much of the extensive literature on the agrarian question continues to build on and advance variants of the teleological, deterministic perspective applied to agricultural development and formulated by early Marxists such as Karl Kautsky, V. I. Lenin, and Rosa Luxemburg (Kautsky 1988; Lenin 1899; Luxemburg 1913). These perspectives often share one or all of the following assumptions: that large-scale capitalist agriculture is more efficient and techno-logically dynamic than "peasant" or non-capitalist agriculture; that non-capitalist forms are, or should be, transitory or are misidentified as non-capitalist; that various obstacles explain the anomalous persistence of the family farm; and that non-capitalist forms serve as a barrier to the unfolding of the "natural" develop-mental path of capitalism in agriculture.

An alternative strain of this literature challenges the underlying deterministic and teleological construction of historical change implicit in other formulations of the agrarian question, and builds on the work of A. V. Chayanov, who argued that the family farm (or peasant mode of production) is an efficient, competitive agricultural institution, whose distinctive features could allow it to survive in the midst of capitalism. In particular, Chayanov argued that the unpaid labor of farm family members, and their willingness to increase their "rate of self-exploitation" in order to survive in times of crisis, could enable peasant family farms to compete with and overcome large-scale capitalist units (Chayanov 1986). (See, for example, Reinhardt and Barlett 1989; McLaughlin 1998 for a survey of this literature.)

Following Chayanov, I theorize the family farm as a stable, technologically dynamic class structural form in U.S. agriculture. I proceed from a conception of agricultural development and the place of the family farm in which there is no predetermined, necessary path of historical movement, but only the complex, contradictory, open-ended, and overdetermined result of the interactions of con-crete historical processes. I theorize the family farm as a complex hybrid of mostly feudal and ancient class structures in its constituent components – the farm enterprise and the farm household. Shaped by ideological processes that define the primacy of the ancient as the "farmer" and of the ancient class struc-ture in the farm enterprise as "farming," it has been subsidized by the feudal exploitation of the family farm's women and children, by the cannibalization of neighboring ancient farmers in a vicious hunt for super profits, and by the inter-vention of state welfare programs directed toward ancient farmers.

This analysis of the family farm, its transformation, and its survival is one that is more nuanced than the deterministic variants of the story about the "death of the family farm" and "the transition to capitalism." The twentieth century wit-nessed dramatic changes in the family farm's class structures and their con-ditions of existence, yet the family farm, a mostly non-capitalist entity, still survived, and in many cases flourished, even though that survival came at the expense of family members and one or more of the family farm's constituent class structures, at the expense of neighboring farmers, and at the expense of taxpayers. Nostalgia for the family farm of the past has now been exposed as nostalgia, in part, for a particular form of serfdom, for a form of the family farm hybrid that relied on long hours of hard work, dependence, and exploitation of women and children in the context of the family farm's feudal class structures. Shifts in the family farm's subsidization strategies signaled not its extinction, but its continued survival as a non-capitalist entity partly enabled by the rise of capitalism in agriculture. Family farm members may have increasingly experienced capitalist class exploitation in their participation in non-farm class processes, and capitalist class processes may have grown in non-farm agricultural enterprises, but the family farm remained in many ways impervious to the growth of capitalist class structures, despite their growing importance elsewhere in the agricultural system. Experiments with the capitalist "bonanza" wheat farms in the late nineteenth century highlighted the particular advantages of the non-capitalist hybrid form, as the capitalist corporations lacked the ability to exploit the unpaid labor of family members to maximize surplus and minimize costs in response to falling agricultural prices. Aside, perhaps, from some hired hands on family farms, capitalist class processes have remained largely absent from actual farm production, having retreated from initial inroads by the turn of the twentieth century. The twentieth century process of "capitalist integration" may well have strengthened both capitalist and non-capitalist class structures in agriculture – the former in the non-farm agricultural economy and the latter in farming itself. Ancient and feudal structures appear to have persisted in millions of family farms, aided by the flexibility of the hybrid form which, while multiplying crisis points, also multiplied possible strategies for responding to crisis. In this way, the strengthening of capitalism in the non-farm agricultural economy has relied upon the continued existence and strengthening of non-capitalist class structures in farm production itself, and vice versa.

In addition, the class-based definition of the family farm yields unique insights into three broad aspects of U.S. agricultural history. First, this analysis highlights the crucial, yet under-recognized and under-examined role of farm women and children's unpaid labor in the survival of the family farm. While the family farm depended for its survival on the exploitation of all farm family members, the primacy of the ancient class structures rendered the feudal class structures and their importance, along with the hybrid form of the family farm, largely invisible. I have argued for the crucial role of women's "invisible" labor in the survival of the family farm, and examined the conflicts stemming from that role. The contradictory implication is that farm women's feudal dependence both supported and undermined the ancient farmer's "independence." Although not recognized as such, the successful exploitation of farm women within the feudal class structures of the family farm generated the backlash to that arrangement and its accompanying burden of long hours of strenuous work, isolation, and subordination that many farm women shouldered. Concern for the impacts of that rebellion on the health of rural society found expression during the early twentieth century in the Country Life Movement, and what became known as the "farm woman problem."

In highlighting women's role in family farms, I join the conversation with feminist historians of rural women's history, to whom my work is indebted (for example, Jensen 1981; Sachs 1983; Fink 1986; Elbert 1987; Fink 1992; Jellison 1993; Neth 1998; Osterud 2012). I contribute the added dimension of class to that literature on the question of women's "liberation" and its relationship to things like women's participation in farm and household labor processes, access to technology, political empowerment, and other factors commonly debated and discussed. I argue that the dimension of class adds to the richness of our explanations and enhances our understanding of how women's struggles for justice succeed or fail. Political processes of gender-based oppression shape and are shaped by economic processes of class exploitation. For example, whether or not changes in women's access to labor saving technologies in home production, or in their participation in farm production processes, is empowering is conditioned by a variety of factors including ethnicity, socioeconomic status, familial relationships, educational attainment, etc. One of those factors includes their position in exploitative class processes. I emphasize the role of class not because it is more important than these other factors, but because it, unlike them, has been overlooked in the existing literature. Just as farm women failed to recognize or speak about their dilemmas in terms of class and so failed to resolve the farm woman problem, we as scholars also fail to comprehend these dilemmas if we do not include an awareness and language of class in our explanations.

Second, I offer a new, class-based perspective on the roots of the twentieth century "miracle of productivity" in U.S. agriculture, the rise of the agribusiness giants that depended on the perpetual, technology-induced crisis of that agriculture, and the implications of the seemingly infinite largesse of the U.S. government toward family farmers. Beginning in the 1920s with the adoption of the farm tractor, and accelerating thereafter, processes of technical change shifted U.S. agriculture onto a new trajectory of development toward the industrial agriculture model we are familiar with today. The change was accompanied by severe economic distress and rural dislocation as millions of family farms suffered ongoing crisis and failure. The 1920s and 30s were periods of particularly sustained crisis and, as a result, the 1930s marked the beginning of unprecedented government intervention in the agricultural economy. After having nearly ground to a halt between 1900 and 1920, productivity growth took off, particularly after 1935. During the post-World War II expansion of U.S. capitalism, no other sector outperformed agriculture in terms of productivity growth. In severe decline and subject to massive government intervention, non-capitalist family farms became the most technologically dynamic enterprises in the United States.

My analysis adds a new, class-based understanding of these developments. In a sense, improved farm productivity through technical change, driven in part by the competitive struggle among family farmers, became an answer to the limits of class exploitation within the family farm, while also generating contradictory outcomes. The internal subsidies from family farm members were supplemented by those from outside the family farm – from other farmers in the form of super profits, and from the state in the form of price supports and other farm programs. Like the feudal class structures within the family farm, these helped the ancient farmer transcend the limits of auto-exploitation, maximizing the revenues available without overtaxing his physical capabilities and threatening his ability to reproduce his own labor power. The few successful farmers cannibalized their neighbors and swallowed their assets, while the rural landscape became increasingly littered with the failed farms of the losers and the crumbling communities they left behind. The very success of ancient competition pushed the state into providing welfare to all those who participated directly in this competitive struggle. All of these developments helped fuel the rise of capitalist agribusiness depending on and enabling both the continuous process of crisis-induced (and inducing) technical change, as well as the state welfare to ancient farmers keeping the technology treadmill going.

A third outcome of this analysis is to show how the unique set of contradictions and circumstances facing family farmers at this time, including class exploitation, were connected to concern for their ability to serve the needs of U.S. industrial capitalist development. The farm woman problem itself was part of a broader concern with "backward" agriculture stemming from the stagnant agricultural productivity growth and resulting high food prices during the early twentieth century. Agricultural development was an issue of the utmost national concern during the early twentieth century. The hunt for super profits, combined with farm programs, produced the combination of cheap food, a vast supply of workers from the countryside, and an expanding market for industrial goods in rural areas that proved a potent formula for economic development. It contributed to a rising rate of class exploitation in industry while supporting the real wage. These developments helped foster the post-war economic boom, and catapulted U.S. agriculture to global dominance, but came at the expense of the intensified exploitation of farm families and massive dislocation in the countryside as millions of family farms collapsed.

As the world again faces the specter of Malthusian-style food shortages and perpetually rising food prices, as well as the human and environmental degradation associated with the industrial agriculture model, my work is particularly instructive. The U.S. model is often advanced as a formula for agricultural development elsewhere in the world, and more industrialization is touted as the solution to agricultural problems in the developed world as well. My perspective contrasts with the view that technical change in U.S. agriculture has represented efficiency, and that the dislocation suffered by farmers and rural communities is the necessary price to pay for progress. From a Marxian perspective, the development of exploitative class structures thus enabled signals a crime wave of social theft, and is hardly something to be celebrated as "progress." The expansion of the food supply necessary to sustain the population might have been accomplished without inflicting such trauma on that same population, and could still. Moreover, the overdeterminist view of technical change means there can be no necessity or inevitability attached to any set of technical innovations or agricultural institutions associated with them. The idea that the particular circumstances that produced this "success" in the U.S. will prevail elsewhere, as some sort of formula for agricultural development is also called into question.

In the struggle over the future course of global agricultural development, I add my voice to those who advocate a turn toward an alternative model of the agrifood system. My work highlights the social and personal costs associated with the intensification of exploitation in the transition to industrial agriculture in the U.S. In addition, my work implicates the beloved family farm in this social theft. This analysis presents a family farm that is quite different from the mythical ideal. Rather than preserving the sanctity of the traditional and celebrated rural family, the family farmer instead participates in hastening its demise. Rather than embodying the spirit of neighborliness and local community, the family farmer instead participates in hastening his neighbors' demise. And finally, instead of being the self-reliant, independent, rugged individual producer, he is one of the nation's longest-lived, and least recognized, "welfare queens."

Ironically, the same family farm is often held up as the political, economic, and cultural bedrock of American life. Its exalted status as an example of democracy, independence, self-sufficiency, and morality is enabled among other things by the absence of class awareness in U.S. society. Indeed, the family farm may well be an example, albeit of something quite different than its celebrants generally understand, for in what other industry could the labor of men, women, and children be so fully exploited and the exploitation thereby of others so successfully enabled? When viewed through the lens of class, the hallowed family farm is an example of one of the most exploitative institutions in the U.S. economy. The myth of its superiority takes on a new significance as one of the important non-economic processes helping to overdetermine the family farm's long survival, while participating in foreclosing truly radical transformations of these institutions to non-exploitative alternatives. By bringing the class perspective to light, my research highlights the pitfalls of this nostalgia for the family farm of the past, and helps point the way toward a truly democratic food system for the future.

References

Chayanov A. V. 1966 [1925]. "On The Theory of Peasant Economy." In *A. V. Chayanov on The Theory of Peasant Economy*, edited by Daniel Thorner, Basile Kerblay, and R. E. F. Smith. Madison: University of Wisconsin Press.

Elbert, Sarah. 1987. "The Farmer Takes a Wife: Women in America's Farming Families." In *Women, Households, and the Economy*, edited by Lourdes Beneria and Catharine Stimpson, 173–197. New Brunswick and London: Rutgers University Press.

Fink, Deborah. 1986. *Open Country, Iowa: Rural Women, Tradition and Change*. Albany: State University of New York Press.

Fink, Deborah. 1992. *Agrarian Women: Wives and Mothers in Rural Nebraska, 1880–1940*. Studies in Rural Culture. Chapel Hill and London: University of North Carolina Press.

Gabriel, Satyananda. 1990. "Ancients: A Marxian Theory of Self-Exploitation." *Rethinking Marxism* 3 (1): 85–106.

Jellison, Katherine. 1993. *Entitled to Power*. Chapel Hill: University of North Carolina Press.

Jensen, Joan. 1981. *With These Hands : Women Working on the Land*. Old Westbury, NY: Feminist Press.

Kautsky, Karl. 1988. *The Agrarian Question: In Two Volumes*. London and Winchester, MA: Zwan Publications.

Lenin, V. I. 1899. *The Development of Capitalism in Russia*. Marxists Internet Archive. Available online at www.marxists.org/archive/lenin/works/1899/devel/.

Luxemburg, Rosa. 1913. *The Accumulation of Capital.* Marxists Internet Archive. Available online at www.marxists.org/archive/luxemburg/1913/accumulation-capital/.

McLaughlin, Paul. 1998. "Rethinking the Agrarian Question: The Limits of Essentialism and the Promise of Evolutionism." *Human Ecology Review* 5 (2): 25–39.

Neth, Mary C. 1998. *Preserving the Family Farm: Women, Community, and the Foundations of Agribusiness in the Midwest, 1900–1940.* Baltimore: The Johns Hopkins University Press.

Osterud, Grey. 2012. *Putting the Barn Before the House: Women and Family Farming in Early Twentieth-Century New York.* Ithaca: Cornell University Press.

Reinhardt, Nola, and Peggy Barlett. 1989. "The Persistence of Family Farms in United States Agriculture." *Sociologia Ruralis* 29 (3–4) (December 1): 203–225.

Resnick, Stephen, and Richard Wolff. 1979. "The Theory of Transitional Conjunctures and the Transition from Feudalism to Capitalism in Western Europe." *Review of Radical Political Economics* 11 (30): 3–22.

Sachs, Carolyn E. 1983. *The Invisible Farmers: Women in Agricultural Production.* Totowa, NJ: Rowman & Allanheld.

Sweezy, Paul, et al. 1992. *The Transition from Feudalism to Capitalism.* London: Verso.

Appendix A

The hunt for super profits

The hunt for super profits without state price supports

Step 1: Before innovation

Consider three ancient farm enterprises as alike in terms of value flows. Each ancient uses $4 worth of C, pays himself $2 of V and self-appropriates $2 of S. The total corn produced is 3 bushels, divided equally among the three ancient producers. I assume that one abstract hour = 1 dollar so that each ancient works for 4 hours and thus the technical productivity of each is UV/LL = ¼ where UV = use value(s) and LL = living labor

	C	V	S	W	r	occ	ac
Farmer #1	4	2	2	8	1/3	2/3	6
Farmer #2	4	2	2	8	1/3	2/3	6
Farmer #3	4	2	2	8	1/3	2/3	6

Where:

C = constant capital
V = variable capital
S = surplus
W = value
r = value profit rate (S/(C+V))
occ = organic composition of capital (C/(C+V))
ac = average cost ((C+V)/UV)

The unit value (W/UV) in the corn industry is the social average or 24/3 = $8. This represents in labor hours the socially necessary abstract labor time of 8 hours to produce a bushel of corn.

Step 2: After innovation

Suppose Ancient #2 purchases a tractor that raises the technical productivity on his farm. He can apply less LL and produce the same number of UV, or the same LL and produce more UV. Assume he is able to expand land under corn cultivation so that his LL is still 4 hours. I will assume that $4 more of C is purchased, and that it enables another unit of corn to be produced with the same LL. Ancient #2 therefore raises the productivity on his farm enterprise from 1/4 to 2/4. The new value flows are as follows:

	C	V	S	W	r	occ	ac
Farmer #1	4	2	2	8	2/6	2/3	6
Farmer #2	8	2	2	12	2/10	4/5	5
Farmer #3	4	2	2	8	2/6	2/3	6

The new social unit value, the weighted average across the three ancient producers, to produce a bushel of corn is 28/4 = $7. Farmer #2 now has a private value of 12/2 = $6.

Assuming that each producer must sell at the socially determined price equal to unit value, new revenues (R), costs, and profits for each become the following:

	R	C + V	Market Profit	Market Profit Rate
Farmer #1	7	6	1	1/6
Farmer #2	14	10	4	4/10
Farmer #3	7	6	1	1/6

Super profits are now transferred from less to more productive farmers as follows:

$$NCR_{SP} = \left(\left(\frac{W}{UV}\right) - \left(\frac{W}{UV}\right)_{PR}\right) \times UV$$

Ancient farmer #2 gets a super profit ($NCR_{SP} > 0$) which is equal to the difference between the social unit value and his lower private unit value, or (7–6) * 2 = $2. He captures that super profit at the direct expense of ancient farmers #1 and #3. His $NCR_{SP} > 0$ is the consequence of $NCR_{SP} < 0$ for farmers #1 and #3, where $\Sigma NCR_{SP} = 0$. Ancient farmer #2 is now the low cost producer of corn and can earn a higher market profit rate by increasing his occ.

Step 3: Imitation and diffusion

Farmers #1 and #3 now face the following situation in ancient corn production:

$$S(A) - NCR_{SP} < SSCP(A)$$

Farmers #1 and #3 must respond in some way, or risk death as ancient farmers. One possible strategy is to avoid losing S by copying the innovating strategy of #2. Widespread diffusion of the new technology (in this case, the tractor), alters value flows and profits as follows:

	C	V	S	W	r	occ	ac
Farmer #1	8	2	2	12	1/5	4/5	5
Farmer #2	8	2	2	12	1/5	4/5	5
Farmer #3	8	2	2	12	1/5	4/5	5

The new social average unit value is 36/6 = $6. The new amount of corn produced has increased from 3 to 6 bushels. Each producer has raised productivity to 1/2, lowered average costs to $5, and raised the occ. Now, however, each producer earns a lower value (and market) profit rate or 1/5 instead of 1/3 or 2/5 due to the increasing occ. The innovator's lead has been erased as he is no longer siphoning surplus from his less productive competitors. Each ancient farmer's private innovating action has contradictory consequences for them all and for the industry. Intense competition has been shaped by technical change and vice versa, which produces a crisis in corn farming of a falling value rate of profit.

As discussed in the Chapter 3, there are also countervailing tendencies contributing to a rising profit rate. Ancient farmers may pursue other strategies as well. Both imitation and these other strategies will impact the family farm's other class structures, impacting the flows of value between them.

The hunt for super profits with state price supports

Step 1: Innovation

Same as above

Step 2: After innovation

If state intervention supports the price farmers receive for corn at the initial (before innovation) social unit value of $8, the initial innovation (the purchase of a tractor) would have the following impact on revenues and market profits (assume the impact on value flows is as presented in Step 2 above):

	R	C + V	Market Profit	Market Profit Rate
Farmer #1	8	6	2	1/3
Farmer #2	16	10	6	3/5
Farmer #3	8	6	2	1/3

Farmer #2 gets the $NCR_{SP} = (7–6) * 2 = 2 as before from Farmers #1 and #3.

In addition, all farmers receive a transfer from the state,

$$NCR_{FMV} = \left(P_{FMV} - \left(\frac{W}{UV} \right) \right) \times UV$$

$NCR_{FMV} = (8{-}7) * UV = \$1 * UV$. Farmer #2 therefore receives a larger share of state payments (\$2) based on his larger production (2 bushels). Farmers #1 and #3 each receive \$1 from the state, which exactly offsets what each is losing to Farmer #2. This is because the private unit value for Farmers #1 and #3 is the same as the social unit value before the innovation. Since we assumed that initially prices and values were equal, the government-set price, P_{FMV} , equals $(W/UV)_{PR}$ for farmers who did not innovate. Farmers #1 and #3 are back where they started at Step 1, while Farmer #2 has captured \$2 + \$2 = \$4 in additional revenue. He is now in a superior position to grow his enterprise or otherwise expand his conditions of existence. Whatever strategy he pursues will further impact Farmers #1 and #3, so they still have an incentive to imitate his initial innovation to level the playing field.

State expenditures on supporting the price at \$8 are \$4 and, as noted, the larger farmer (in terms of production), gets a larger share of those expenditures. Instead of the previous \$6, there is now \$10 available for farmers to distribute toward securing their conditions of existence.

Step 3: Imitation

Widespread imitation and diffusion in the context of price supports produces the same value flows as Step 3 above. However, in this case, revenues and market profits are as follows:

	R	C + V	Market Profit	Market Profit Rate
Farmer #1	16	10	6	3/5
Farmer #2	16	10	6	3/5
Farmer #3	16	10	6	3/5

As above, the social unit value has fallen to \$6, but the price farmers receive is \$8. There are no transfers of super profits anymore, as they all have the same productivity and private unit value. However, there are dramatically increased transfers from the state to support the price of the increased output, which is now even farther above the unit value.

$NCR_{FMV} = (8{-}6) * 2 = \$4$ for each farmer, not just for the innovator. The entire \$4 is the result of a transfer from the state. State expenditures to support the price at \$8 are now \$12.

State expenditures have ballooned, as has the revenue available for farmers to distribute to secure their conditions of existence. Instead of \$6, there is now \$18 available. The state has financed an increasing occ along with an increase in the mass and rate of profit in corn farming.

Appendix B

The story of hybrid corn

The second major agricultural development of the early twentieth century was the invention and rapid adoption of hybrid corn. Hybrids are the result of cross-breeding different varieties of inbred, or self-pollinated, lines of corn. The first generation of hybrid plants exhibits what is called heterosis, or "hybrid vigor" – producing yields greater than the parent plants. But the seeds of the first generation hybrids don't "come true." That is, yields decline dramatically with the second generation, making the seeds of the first generation plants virtually worthless. This characteristic is referred to as a "genetically closed pedigree." Instead of farmers being able to select and save their own seed from the previous year's crop, as they commonly did, they had to return to the seed company every year to purchase the new hybrid seeds and the increased yields they offered.

In the early twentieth century, corn was the dominant field crop in the United States and a major focus of plant breeding research efforts. Farmers had cultivated and improved it for millennia using selective breeding, or choosing individual ears of corn on the basis of appearance and saving the seeds for the following year's crop. Corn was open-pollinated, meaning farmers relied on natural cross-pollination between plants. Accidental hybridization occurred, as did deliberate cross-variety breeding. Reid's Yellow Dent, the most popular open-pollinated variety of the time was one of these "varietal hybrids," but none of these was a "true" hybrid of inbred lines.

Working separately with single-crossed inbred lines, both George Shull and Edward East demonstrated hybrid vigor – the hybrid offspring produced higher yields than the inbred parent plants. Their results were published in 1908. Donald F. Jones was the first to demonstrate the commercial viability of hybridization in 1918 with the invention of the "double-cross inbred hybrid corn," the type of hybrid that launched the industry. All of these early efforts occurred through publicly funded breeding programs. Throughout the 1920s and early 1930s, however, hybridization remained only one of many ideas about how to improve corn, and was in many ways the least promising. Early hybrids were temperamental, required extremely fertile soil, and thrived in limited geographic areas (Fitzgerald 1993). Massive government intervention, aggressive marketing campaigns, and an accident of weather helped tip the balance by reducing the costs of development and adoption (Sutch 2008).

In 1921, Henry C. Wallace became Secretary of Agriculture, and at the urging of his son, Henry A. Wallace, an avid corn breeder, phased out the USDA's traditional corn breeding program and established a new Bureau of Plant Industry to research hybrids. While Henry A. used *Wallace's Farmer* to "educate" farmers about the benefits of the new hybrids, he continued to work on developing his own variety. After several failed attempts to outperform open pollinated varieties with hybrids in the Iowa Corn Yield Tests, his "Copper Cross" won in 1924. Wallace produced "Copper Cross" from two parental lines developed by public breeding programs. One was from the Connecticut Experiment Station, and the other from the federal corn breeding program his father had established. In 1926, Wallace founded Pioneer Hi-Bred, the first commercial hybrid seed corn company. "Copper Cross" sold for a whopping $52 a bushel, to "convince farmers they were buying something special" (Sutch 2008). Funk Brothers, a leading seed company at the time, introduced its first double cross hybrid in 1928. Several new companies began production within a few years. In 1929, J. Sidney Cates declared in the pages of *Country Gentleman* that "the day of super-corn has come.... This work, in short, comes nearer to making evolution stand on its hind legs and bark like a dog than anything yet accomplished with an economic plant" (Cates 1929, 20). Buried on the last page of the article was the part about how hybrids could not be saved for replanting and maintain their superior performance. Instead, they had to be purchased anew each year from the seed company. Cates's enthusiasm (and his attempt to bury the bad news) notwithstanding, farmers remained unconvinced. Not only was the new crop expensive to adopt, but risky as well. Potential crop failure was devastating, and unlike their open-pollinated cousins which came in a wide variety of shapes, sizes, and colors, the new seeds offered no outward visual signs to indicate their performance in a particular farmer's field. Companies like Pioneer offered substantial discounts, but these were offered only to a select few farmers in each locale. For most farmers, the yield gains simply were not enough to make the new hybrid worthwhile.

By 1933, hybrid corn cultivation remained at less than 1 percent of planted acreage. Then came the drought of 1934, and devastating crop failures throughout the Corn Belt. One of Pioneer's experimental hybrid varieties, number 307, remained standing. This accidental discovery became a goldmine when the second drought hit in 1936, the same year Hybrid 307 was introduced commercially. Even though hybrids were not clearly superior under normal growing conditions, in demonstrating an undeniable edge in averting complete crop failure, hybrids finally overcame farmers' resistance. Wallace demonstrated his unwavering commitment to promoting the new, scientific agriculture by devoting the 1936 *Yearbook of Agriculture*, the annual report of the Department's activities distributed widely to Congress and the public, to "a single subject – the creative development of new forms of life through plant and animal breeding" (Sutch 2008, 18). By around 1940, seed companies had stopped selling open-pollinated varieties and, by 1945, 90 percent of corn acreage was planted with hybrid corn (Fitzgerald 1993, 340).

References

Cates, J. Sidney. 1929. "The Day of Super Corn Crops." *Country Gentleman.* March.

Fitzgerald, Deborah. 1993. "Farmers Deskilled: Hybrid Corn and Farmers' Work." *Technology and Culture* 34 (2) (April): 324–343. doi:10.2307/3106539.

Sutch, Richard. 2008. "Henry Agard Wallace, The Iowa Corn Yield Tests, And The Adoption Of Hybrid Corn." University of California at Riverside, Department of Economics. Available online at http://ideas.repec.org/p/ucr/wpaper/200807.html.

Index

Page numbers in *italics* denote tables, those in **bold** denote figures.

responsibilities 33–9, *41*; decline in home production activities 119–20; distribution of hours per week for home-making *35*; "double job" 38; economic contribution 38–9, 54, 61; exploitation of 61–2, 74; as feudal appropriators of children's labour 50; feudal perspective 40–2; gathering berries **37**; impact of hired labour on the workload of 68–9, 91; impact of mechanization on 119–21; labour considered as feudal 26; leisure time 70; and marriage 33; maternity practices 51, 70; primary occupation 33; seasonal demands **72**; studies 33–4, 36; time devoted to laundry 36–7; undervaluation of work of 15, 76–7, 90; workday for 71
"Farm Women Find Life Hard" (*New York Times*) 15
The Farmer's Wife, "helping out" cover **44**
farming, as virtuous occupation 52–3
"Feminism on the Farm" (*The Nation*) 15
fertilizer market, tractors and the expansion of the 98
feudal-ancient subsidies: helping out 63–70; making do 59–63
feudal budget, inequality 63
feudal class structure/process: vs. ancient 54–5, 57–8, 131; children as serfs 42–51; exploitative nature 4 (*see also* feudal exploitation); and family farm production 9; gendered perspective 42; and hired labour 77; historical perspective 3–4; location 8–9; manor economy of medieval Europe 5–6; and mechanization 118–21; in the medieval manor 5; and the mythology of agrarianism 53; offsetting transfers from 60–1, 69; reinforcement by rural institutions 58; subsidization of ancient structure through 59–70; support for ancient class processes 30; in a typical family farm 6–7, 26, 42, 130–2
feudal exploitation 6, 8, 42, 57, 60, 91, 122, 130–1
feudal revenues, of the family farm 26
feudal surplus 26, 60–1, 63, 67; sources 63
feudal surplus labour, of farm women 26–7
feudalism, gender-based 4
field work: done by children 46–7; done by women 35, 39, 64; number of hours done by children *47*; typical duration 47
Fink, D. 53–4, 66
Fitzgerald, D. 114

food, cheap 11, 20, 102, 133
Fraad, H. 4
the frontier 91
fundamental class process, Marxian theory 3
fundamental class processes, in the medieval manor 6

Gabriel, S. 3–5, 10, 29, 129
Galpin, J. 50, 56
Garland, H. 45
gender, and the delineation of responsibility 40
Glaspell, S. 79
Golden Age period 11, 91, 101
Gray, G. 71
Great Depression 86–8, 100–1, 103, 107, 120
growth, immiserizing 101

Harding, Warren G. 89
harvesters 27
helping out 27, 40, **44**, 54, 59, 63–70, 121
Hindess, B. 3
hired labour 7, 15, 40, 45–6, 50, 55, 60, 64–70, 77, 91, 117–19, 131
Hirst, P.Q. 3
home-making, distribution of hours per week for *35*
Homestead Act (1862) 33
horse-powered combine, horse- and man-power requirements 118
horse-powered farm machinery, introduction of 92
horses, and the farm crisis 94
hours of work, of ancient farmers 30
household feudalism, gender-based 4, 42
household size, rural average 67
housework: gendered perspective 55–6; men's contributions 76–7; perceived status 56
hybrid, definition 5
hybrid class structure, concept analysis 5
hybrid corn, mechanization and the adoption of 92, 109, 139, 140–2
hybrid seed 92

immiserizing growth 101
implement manufacturers: market power 112–13; monopoly practices 113
industrial agriculture, arrival of 87
industrialization: impact on all aspects of crop production 87; impacts on farmers and their families 88; and the "New Agriculture" 88

inheritance patterns 57
internal combustion engine 87, 92–3
isolation 12–14, 51, 58, 62, 67, 91, 131; of
the ancient farmer 29–30; of farm
women and children 57–8

Jefferson, T. 52, 54
Jellison, K. 120
Jones, N.K. 36

Kautsky, K. 129
Kayatekin, S.A. 4
King, W. 94
Kleinegger, C. 54
Kneeland, H. 34
Knowles, J. 63
Korean War 115

labour, distributions of **32**
labour hours, per 100 bushels of corn **86**
labour-saving technology 13, 15, 20, 29,
35, 37, 62–3, 70, 74, 90, 119–20, 122
land ownership 29
land prices, impact of World War I 89
laundry, hours per week spent on 36–7
leisure time 30, 34, 55, 70
Lenin, V.I. 129
Levin, K. 5
Lighthall, D.R. 88
livestock 5, 24–5, 27, 30–2, 39, 41, 45, 50,
60, 64–5, 117, 119
living standards of farm families, role of
women's household production 39
loan rate 105, 107, 115–16
Lovett, L.L. 53
Luxemburg, R. 129

McCormick, Cyrus 92, 95
McCormick, Fowler 95
MacKaye, B. 88
making do 27, 59–63, 64, 67
manor economy of medieval Europe,
feudal class structure 5–6
marriage, farm women and 33
Marxian perspectives 2–5, 7, 14, 95, 100,
102, 129
mechanization: and class crisis 99; debate
on the social desirability 94–5; and the
decline in farm employment 117–18;
and the decline in numbers of farmers
99; impact on food supplies 100–1;
impact on profits 100, 101–2; impact on
women's and children's work 119;
launch of second phase 92;

transformation of labour processes
116–17; *see also* tractors
mischievous idle hands, warning against
the dangers of 43
Mitchell, E.B. 69, 77
modern conveniences 54, 74–5, 119
Moore, Hiram 92
Murphy, Z. 121

necessary labour, definition 3
Neth, M.C. 38–9, 55, 64
New Deal 93, 95, 104, 107, 119

Olmstead, A.L. 93, 100
outmigration, from rural areas 77, 88; *see
also* rural flight

parity 91, 101, 115, 125
Parket, W.N. 88
patroonships, Dutch system 1
production cooperatives 90
pronatalism, coercive 56
Purnell Act (1925) 34

Quick, H. 12, 24

Rankin, J.O. 43, 45, 71
record-keeping, women's responsibilities
62
Resnick, S. 2, 4
revenues, transfer of 9
"The Revolt of Mother" (Wilkins) 16
"Revolt of the Farmer's Wife" (Bruère/
Bruère) 14
Rhode, P.W. 93, 100
right to childhood, recognition of 49, 51
Roberts, R. S. 88
Roosevelt, Theodore 11–12, 54, 56
rural flight 12–13, 74, 77
rural to urban migration, post-war
acceleration 100
rural uplift 12–13, 18, 89

sacrifice, necessity of 55
school, rural attendance 75
seeds, devaluation of farmers' skill with
breeding and selecting 114
self-exploitation 3–5, 10, 60–1
serfs, children as 42–51
set-aside 115
sharecropping 2, 4
single women 33
slavery 2
Smith Lever Act (1914) 62

For Product Safety Concerns and Information please contact our EU
representative GPSR@taylorandfrancis.com
Taylor & Francis Verlag GmbH, Kaufingerstraße 24, 80331 München, Germany

www.ingramcontent.com/pod-product-compliance
Ingram Content Group UK Ltd.
Pitfield, Milton Keynes, MK11 3LW, UK
UKHW021826240425
457818UK00006B/96